Problem Solving in All Seasons

Prekindergarten–Grade 2

Kim Markworth,
Jenni McCool, and Jennifer Kosiak

NATIONAL COUNCIL OF
TEACHERS OF MATHEMATICS

www.nctm.org/more4u
Access code: PAS14808

Library of Congress Cataloging-in-Publication Data

Markworth, Kim.
  Problem solving in all seasons, prekindergarten–grade 2 / Kim Markworth, Jenni McCool,
and Jennifer Kosiak.
      pages cm
Includes bibliographical references.
  ISBN 978 0 87353 771 1
  1. Mathematics Study and teaching (Preschool) 2. Mathematics Study and teaching (Early
childhood) 3. Mathematics Study and teaching (Primary) I. McCool, Jenni. II. Kosiak, Jennifer, 1972 III. Title.
  QA135.6.M3635 2015
  372.7'049 dc23

                                    2015019001

The National Council of Teachers of Mathematics is the public voice of mathematics
education, supporting teachers to ensure equitable mathematics learning of the highest quality
for all students through vision, leadership, professional development, and research.

Printed in the United States of America

Contents

PREFACE

The purpose of this book is to provide challenging and engaging problem-solving tasks for children in the primary years. All children are aware of seasons and holidays, and these provide authentic and engaging backgrounds for the problems. These tasks can be easily related to other topics and themes that are being studied and discussed in the classroom, providing occasions for cross-disciplinary connections.

The situations in this book provide occasions in which children can engage in content on a problem-solving level. Each problem is tied to at least one Common Core content standard at a particular grade level. Consider these problem-solving tasks as opportunities for children to explore strategies and make sense of important mathematics. Allowing children time and freedom to engage in this kind of sense making, reasoning, justification, and pattern searching provides them the openings to engage in the Common Core State Standards for Mathematical Practice. Thus, we see these tasks as invitations for children to learn important mathematical ideas in relevant contexts as they engage in the mathematical practices that are at the heart of the Common Core State Standards for Mathematics (CCSSM).

WHAT TO EXPECT IN THE FOLLOWING PAGES

The Introduction provides a discussion of problem solving that sets the stage for the tasks and the implementation guide that is provided for each one. The book has four chapters organized by season: fall, winter, spring, and summer. Each of these chapters includes two problem-solving tasks for each grade level; these are arranged in grade-level order from prekindergarten to second grade.

We hope that teachers find some flexibility for differentiation by using problems at different grade levels. If a situation for the children's grade level seems too challenging or too simplistic, alternatives may be found by examining—and potentially adapting—the tasks for other grade levels.

We also hope that teachers take advantage of the ability to alter the contexts of the problems to better suit their local circumstances. However, we urge caution with manipulating tasks. It is easy to change aspects of a situation that remove the challenge of engaging in relevant and meaningful mathematics. Be sure to maintain the mathematical core of the tasks themselves, preserving children's opportunities to struggle through the mathematics.

Each lesson is comprised of several components. Blackline masters as well as other materials for each task are available for downloading and printing on NCTM's More4U online resource (nctm.org/more4u). The teacher may find that a handout is unnecessary at times, especially with emerging readers. Instead, the worksheet may be used as a class display, and students may be encouraged to use alternatives for recording their work.

The discussion of each problem provides the primary content standards and mathematical practices from CCSSM that students can be expected to employ as they work through the task. When CCSSM content standards are not available—as is the case with prekindergarten students—*Principles and Standards for School Mathematics* (NCTM 2000) and other resources are referenced for important mathematical concepts. The Problem Discussion provides greater detail about the mathematics of the task and ways in which mathematical practices are employed as children solve the problem. Understanding the mathematics is important, and we hope that the problem discussion for each task effectively highlights the mathematical ideas around which each task is structured.

Sections on Strategies and Misconceptions/Student Difficulties identify potential student solution strategies and the challenges and misconceptions they may encounter through the problem. Following these sections is a detailed description of how students might engage in the task using the Launch/Explore/Summarize format. In each of these sections, we have featured ways to apply the characteristics of the three-phase lesson format in relation to the specific task.

Finally, a section on Differentiation identifies ways in which a task may be expanded or simplified for the variety of learners found in any classroom. Children should be provided with ample time to make sense of and engage in the problems. For children who derive a solution quickly, this section offers suggestions for how their thinking regarding the particular content might be deepened. For others who are unable to engage in *productive struggle* with the task, the section provides suggestions for modifying the task without significantly reducing the children's opportunity to engage in mathematical reasoning.

What to Expect in the Online Components

The online components for this book include a Microsoft Word version of problem handouts as well as other materials associated with each problem, such as figure cutouts, ten-frames, and task cards. The Word version of the handout can be used to change names of the characters in the tasks so children may make a more personal connection to problem situations. Similarly, changes can be easily made to the contexts of the problems so they are more relevant to children's local environments and lives.

Thank you for your interest in this book. We hope that it is a valuable resource to you and opens the door for your students to rich and engaging problem solving!

INTRODUCTION

What does it mean to problem solve? People of all ages engage in problem solving. A toddler might investigate how to obtain a toy that is just out of her reach. An adolescent might need to determine how to juggle multiple obligations, responsibilities, and desires effectively. Regardless of the task itself, people who engage in problem solving are seeking a solution to a challenging and novel task. They may bring a variety of knowledge to the process, investigate several possible solution strategies, and experience various degrees of success with their methods. They will experience failure, struggle, and triumphs, all of which contribute to their knowledge base for future problem-solving situations.

PROBLEM SOLVING IN MATHEMATICS

These experiences also apply to problem solving in mathematical contexts. Problem solving in mathematics "means engaging in a task for which the solution method is not known in advance" (NCTM 2000, p. 52). This is an important definition to understand. If one is engaging in a routine task for which the solution strategy is already known, then it is not authentic problem solving. Instead, the routine task is an exercise, and the person engaging in the task is simply practicing a process or a skill or applying previous knowledge to a context (Eves 1963; Zietz 1999). Authentic problem solving, by contrast, means that the person must be engaged in developing new mathematical ideas or applying prior knowledge in new ways.

Although this will certainly involve failure, struggle, and successes, perhaps the most important of these is struggle. It is through active grappling with new concepts that we learn mathematics. Hiebert (2003) emphasizes that classrooms that promote students' understanding "allow mathematics to be problematic for students" (p. 54). As teachers, we are tempted to decrease our students' struggle by removing obstacles or showing them the way. However, it is important to realize that removing students' opportunities to struggle simultaneously reduces their opportunities to learn mathematics for understanding.

The Common Core State Standards for Mathematics (NGA Center and CCSSO 2010) has provided both an opportunity and a challenge for teachers to engage their students in mathematical problem solving. Beyond the clearly defined content standards, the Standards for Mathematical Practice (SMP) are a call for changes to classroom instruction such that students are engaging in challenging tasks, persevering through struggle, justifying and explaining their reasoning, and participating in critical and mathematically focused discourse that occurs throughout the classroom community. At all levels (K–12), students are expected to—

1. make sense of problems and persevere in solving them;
2. reason abstractly and quantitatively;
3. construct viable arguments and critique the reasoning of others;
4. model with mathematics;

5. use appropriate tools strategically;

6. attend to precision;

7. look for and make use of structure; and

8. look for and express regularity in repeated reasoning (NGA Center and CCSSO 2010, pp. 6–8).

Authentic problem solving provides opportunities for students to engage in these eight Standards for Mathematical Practice. Problem-solving tasks develop new understanding about particular content, but a student-centered implementation of the task—and some letting go on the part of the teacher—also allows students to develop mathematical processes or habits of mind that are identified by the practice standards. One might think of the content standards as *what* students are learning and the mathematical practices as *how* students are learning or engaging in the content.

Van de Walle (2003) discusses three characteristics of tasks that successfully promote student learning:

1. What is problematic must be the mathematics.

2. Tasks must be accessible to students.

3. Tasks must require justifications and explanations for answers or methods. (pp. 68–69)

Tasks that meet these descriptors present opportunities for students to develop new mathematical ideas; that is, the mathematics will be problematic for them, and there will be struggle. If students have already mastered the relevant content standards, then these tasks may be fun and engaging activities, but they will not be authentic problem-solving experiences.

Certain lesson formats are more conducive to creating problem-solving experiences that promote meaningful mathematics learning. Van de Walle, Karp, and Bay-Williams (2013) advocate for a three-phase lesson format. The three phases include the following:

1. *Getting Ready:* Activate prior knowledge, be sure the problem is understood, and establish clear expectations.

2. *Students Work:* Let go! Notice students' mathematical thinking, offer appropriate support, and provide worthwhile extensions.

3. *Class Discussion:* Promote a mathematical community of learners, listen actively without evaluation, summarize main ideas, and identify future problems. (p. 49)

The Launch/Explore/Summarize terminology used by the Connected Mathematics Project (Lappan et al. 2014) captures the same ideas articulated above and effectively illustrates the progression of participating in mathematics: Activating prior knowledge, engaging in mathematical thinking about a task, and extracting and summarizing the important mathematical ideas. Each of these phases is discussed in more detail in the following sections.

Launch

The Launch portion of a lesson is the teacher's opportunity to engage students in both the context and the mathematical ideas of a task. It is important to draw students into the circumstances of the task; This allows them to have a personal connection with the task, and helps them see how mathematics may be used in different ways in their or the lives of others. Engaging students in the mathematical ideas of the task is important as well, so students have a general understanding of the problem they are to solve.

There are multiple ways to engage students in the context of a task. Perhaps the most simple is to ask, "What do you know about … (e.g., Election Day)?" This kind of broad approach will provide a good sense of where the students are in relation to the context of the problem. It may surface misconceptions, but it may also bring out family traditions that can be shared so students' understanding and respect for others' experiences can be developed. Other questions that might be asked include the following:

- Has anyone here ever been …?
- How many of you like to …?
- How many of you celebrate …?

Sharing of students' beliefs and experiences provides the teacher an opening to add to the conversation, providing more information about the holiday or seasonal event to further connect students to the frame of reference.

Of course, depending on location, there may be very limited experience with the context of a task. If students have never seen snow before, it may be challenging to interest them in a situation about sledding or snowfall. If students have lived their entire lives in an urban setting, they may not bring prior experiences about camping or farming. If this is the case, it is still an excellent occasion to expand students' horizons. Perhaps some students have experience with these less common activities that they can share with the rest of the class. Online pictures and videos are good sources for context development.

Beyond clarifying the context of the task, the Launch is an ideal time to make sure that students understand the problem in which they are about to engage. To do this, students must employ the first Standard of Mathematical Practice, *Make sense of problems and persevere in solving them.* With teacher support, students should establish *what they know* about the problem. This may include knowledge gleaned from the problem itself, such as, "Avery has five friends," or inferences based on the information provided in the problem, such as "Six people will be making valentines." Students may be inclined to dive right into problems, performing operations on the numbers provided without thinking much about the problem itself before doing so. Asking them, "What do you know about this problem?" and listing their responses on a visual display requires them to think about the problem before jumping in.

Students should also be asked to determine *what they want to know.* Their initial focus might be on the answer to the problem. However, there may be questions that emerge as they make sense of the problem that they should be encouraged to recognize as important. Students' identification of these questions helps them realize that the problem solving will not be automatic; they may also be more metacognitively aware of some mental processes they are using while they work toward a solution.

The Launch is also an opportunity for students to develop a tentative plan for solving the problem. This can be tricky to negotiate; students sharing their plans can sometimes funnel other students' thinking at the cost of their own problem-solving strategies. Asking students to share their tentative plans with an elbow partner may alleviate this challenge. Voicing their plans may also help students identify places where their understanding of the task is still limited. Therefore, concluding the conversation with "Does anyone have questions about this problem?" provides a final occasion to clarify the context or the task before they set out to work.

Finally, it is important that students understand how the Explore portion of the lesson will progress. A variety of classroom materials should be made available for their use (e.g., rekenreks, Unifix cubes, color counters, etc.). Although some students may choose not to use manipulatives, these tools offer students who are reasoning less abstractly an entry point to the problems. Students should be assigned to partners or small groups, and be clear on the format expected for a final product.

It is important to note that the Launch portion of the task is not the place where the teacher does a similar problem with students or demonstrates how to solve the problem at hand. Doing either of these may drastically reduce the cognitive demand of the task, students' willingness to engage in the challenge, and the chance to learn important mathematics. While engaging students in preliminary processes for problem solving is necessary, both for tackling the task at hand and developing mathematical practices they can apply to any problem situation, this portion of the lesson should be limited to a meaningful ten minutes that effectively involves students in the context of the problem and the processes that will allow each student access to the problem itself.

EXPLORE

As children engage in these tasks, the teacher's role is to provide appropriate scaffolding without removing students' opportunity to learn. How does a teacher do this? Ask questions. Listen carefully. Assess a child's understanding of the problem and determine where the more challenging aspects lie. Have children talk about their problem-solving strategies: what has worked and what has not.

The Explore portion of a lesson can be the most challenging for teachers who are not accustomed to teaching mathematics through problem solving. As teachers, it is our tendency to want to "help," make the path easier for our students and reduce their struggle. Although we do not want students to get to the point of unproductive frustration, we also need to be cautious about our "helpful" tendencies. Van de Walle's recommendation needs to be taken to heart for this section: "Let go!" (Van de Walle, Karp, and Bay-Williams 2013, p. 49).

Letting go as the students begin working on the task means that they need to be given several minutes to begin tackling the problem. For at least the first several minutes of the Explore portion of a lesson, these student groups or partners should be given the space to continue to process the task, share their initial plans, and begin exploring these plans.

Collaborative work will provide them more ideas for exploration and more insights about how certain mathematical ideas may apply to the task at hand. During this time, the teacher should circulate throughout the room with open ears, simply listening to the immediate challenges and insights. There may be common threads that surface across groups; however, allowing them the time to discuss without intervention may also provide the opportunity for them to resolve misunderstandings and differences.

As students get further in their problem solving, brief visits with each of the groups can keep them moving forward. Ask them questions about their reasoning, such as the following:

- Can you tell me why you decided to do this?
- What does this represent?
- What do you think your next step might be?
- What does this number mean in relation to the problem you're solving?

However, it is important to keep in mind when considering this section of the lesson that the teacher's task is to identify and understand students' mathematical thinking in relation to the task as well as their misconceptions and challenges. This is not possible without close and careful listening to students' discourse.

Task-specific questions or additional support may be necessary for groups that fail to find access into a task. A note of caution, however: This support should not be provided prematurely. Students learn through struggle, and as long as this is not unproductive frustration, they are probably grappling with important ideas and challenges.

Teachers may feel a similar temptation to rescue students who have gotten a wrong answer or are heading down an incorrect path. Again, this struggle is worthwhile, and as long as teachers are open and honest about honoring and respecting the learning that occurs through cognitive dissonance and/or mistakes, then children will see these as valuable learning opportunities as well. This may require a shift in what is honored and emphasized in the mathematics classroom. Processes, strategies, and the longitudinal development of mathematical concepts must be at the core, and mistakes must be valued as learning opportunities by both teachers and students.

Teachers may find it helpful to circulate with a clipboard throughout the Explore portion of the lesson so that misconceptions, challenges, insights, and strategies can be recorded. In many problem-solving lessons, a particular order for sharing strategies in the Summarize portion of the lesson is appropriate. Thus, knowing this order and being able to attend to the students who have reasoned in particular ways is worthwhile for leading students in a productive discussion of the important mathematical ideas related to each task.

Summarize

The Summarize portion of the lesson is the teacher's opportunity to engage the entire class in pulling together essential mathematical ideas. This needs to extend beyond a mere sharing of strategies. Although this is important, it is more important that students have a chance to discuss the mathematical ideas developed in each task, make connections between strategies, identify generalizations when appropriate to do so, and pose new problems.

Students should be exposed to the strategies that were used throughout the classroom community. There are multiple ways to arrange this exposure. Gallery walks, in which students circulate throughout the classroom to observe the work of others, is one effective way to share strategies. Sometimes, it may be appropriate for students to present their strategies to the whole class. At times, it may be important to provide time for everyone to share. Generally, however, we suggest that the choices for sharing be based on the mathematical ideas and strategies utilized by particular groups, with a long-range view of making sure that all students have opportunities to participate in this way. Although students may not have an opportunity in each lesson to present their thinking, they nonetheless ought to be engaged in discussing the strategies that are presented and in making connections between these strategies and their own.

Initially, students may not know how to engage in a community of learners that discusses important mathematical ideas. Although students may focus on nonmathematical ideas at first (e.g., "I like your drawing!"), the teacher can model appropriate probing questions and comments. For example, a teacher might offer comments similar to the following:

- "I'm interested in how you knew that you needed to add these numbers together. Can you explain that?"
- "I see that you used a lot of the same numbers in your problem-solving strategy, although you had a different way of solving the problem. Why do you think we are seeing the same numbers in these places?"
- "How do you think the first group's use of Unifix cubes is similar to your drawing?"
- "I'm not sure I understand what this picture represents. Could you explain that again?"

Students will learn from the teacher's modeling, but there should also be explicit attention to initiating a mathematical discussion. The teacher might ask students to think about the question she just asked and how it helped her clarify her own understanding about the mathematical ideas. The teacher might also consider providing sentence starters to help students structure appropriate and meaningful questions of their own.

It is critical that the mathematical ideas associated with problem-solving tasks be elicited and summarized during the discussion. Anticipating specific questions is helpful, but teachers should also experiment with questions that are particular to the strategies and misconceptions that surface in the classroom. Particular attention can be focused on generalizations that arise from students' thinking. What patterns do they notice? What do they expect would happen with a different set of numbers? What rules can be articulated, either informally or formally?

These generalizations may lead to opportunities for problem posing. Out of many good questions come more questions! Preparation to follow through with students' questions in subsequent problems or to record and post new problems encourages students to think about how these mathematical ideas extend beyond one problem-solving experience. Similarly, if extensions for students have been provided during the Explore phase, students should share the results of these extensions, making deliberate connections to the original task.

In this final discussion, mistakes and misconceptions should be tackled head on. The sharing of incorrect answers may discomfit teachers, but this should be an acceptable experience for students. This requires a safe community of learners in which students are comfortable with risk, expect mistakes to be made, and see opportunity for learning in these mistakes.

As students engage in more and more problem-solving experiences, they should be encouraged to take on more and more of the classroom discourse. Teachers should guide and facilitate rather than manage and direct. Students should be challenged to ask the questions and make the connections. Increasing the number of student comments occurring between teacher comments enables students to increasingly guide the discussion. The teacher needs to know the map, but oftentimes, the students are capable of choosing the route.

Of course, engaging in mathematical discourse like this takes time, effort, and patience. Primary children have plenty of ideas, but have difficulty articulating them. However, the only way to improve discourse is *through* discourse, so teachers should use rich tasks to take risks, and—as one preservice teacher described it—"embrace the train wreck" that may occur when following students' trains of thought. These "train wrecks" can lead to profound learning experiences!

Fall

Fall is the beginning of the school year, but as the leaves turn color, we're reminded that it is harvest time for apples that need to be counted and packaged. From comparing the size of two pumpkins to planning a fall harvest celebration, the tasks in this chapter not only highlight the fall season, but also provide perfect opportunities for meaningful math activities.

Fire Prevention Week inspired the first task. It allows prekindergarten students to investigate location and spatial relationships and gives them the chance to think about an important safety concern in a secure environment. Prekindergarten students will be engaged in comparing pumpkins in the second task by defining and sharing concepts related to measurable attributes of pumpkins.

The two kindergarten tasks focus on important counting strategies to build number sense. The third task uses the context of pumpkins as decorations to investigate addends that sum to eight, while the next task examines counting by twos to determine the number of legs found in a group of turkeys.

In the first grade tasks, students will apply base-ten concepts as they sort apples into bags of ten, as well as geometry concepts related to the partitioning of a gymnasium into halves and fourths for a fall harvest celebration.

The seventh task, "Hay Bales," gives second-grade students the opportunity to reason about even and odd numbers. The last task in this chapter requires students to apply place-value concepts to compare three-digit numbers to determine the winner of an election.

Materials for each task, including handouts, are available for downloading and printing on NCTM's website at nctm.org/more4u by entering the access code on the title page of this book.

Find Two Paths

During Fire Prevention Week, Audrey's teacher asked her to find two paths out of her home. Use the map of Audrey's home to find two paths. Draw each path in a different color. Which path do you think is shorter?

CCSSM Standard for Mathematical Practice

Practice 5: Use appropriate tools strategically.

Standard for Mathematical Content

Students in prekindergarten through second grade should be able to "specify locations and describe spatial relationships using coordinate geometry and other representational systems" (NCTM 2000, p. 96). Specifically, this includes expectations that students of this age—

- "describe, name, and interpret direction and distance in navigating space and apply ideas about direction and distance; [and]
- find and name locations with simple relationships such as 'near to' and in coordinate systems such as maps" (NCTM 2000, p. 96).

Problem Discussion

"Find Two Paths" is a situation that is related to Fire Prevention Week (www.sparky.org), observed during the full week in which October 9th falls (the anniversary of the Great Chicago Fire in 1871). The National Fire Protection Association (NFPA, www.nfpa.org) suggests that children be able to locate two escape routes from each room in their home (routes may include both windows and doors). In this task, students are asked to identify two complete paths from a room in Audrey's home so she can exit her house in case of an emergency.

Clements and Sarama (2009) define spatial orientation as "knowing where you are and how to get around in the world; that is, understanding relationships between different positions in space, at first with respect to your own position and your movement through it, and eventually from a more abstract perspective that includes maps and coordinates" (p. 107). A map, or floor plan, in the case of this task, is an abstract representation of the environment that young children might have difficulty interpreting. However, Clements and Sarama (2009) identify activities appropriate for children of this age that align with the expectations of the task:

- "During free time, challenge children to follow simple maps of the classroom or playground to find secret 'treasures' you have hidden. Interested children can draw their own maps. Start with oblique maps (e.g., in which chairs and tables are shown with legs); [and]
- Walk different routes and discuss different paths, and which would be shorter, which would be longer. Ask *why* one path is shorter" (p. 118).

These suggestions also offer ways in which this task may be enriched by children's exploration of their own space.

In this task, children are asked to find two different routes out of the house from each room. Windows have not been marked, so children are to identify two walking paths that lead to different door exits from Audrey's home. To do this, they will need to make some sense of the floor plan that has been provided (SMP 5). Children may make connections between this map and mazes that they have previously worked with. However, it is likely that children will need some teacher support to make sense of the map and how it relates to a home.

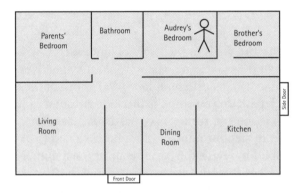

After identifying two different routes for Audrey, children are asked to consider which of these routes is shorter. This is an important concept in relation to its purpose: In case of a real emergency, Audrey would want to exit her house as quickly as possible. Children may have different ways of thinking about this question. They may consider how many rooms or doorways Audrey needs to pass through. They may also consider the actual linear distance of each of the lines. The routes will be challenging to compare because they may not be entirely straight and direct comparison of the lines is not possible. However, children may identify ways to compare the paths by visual estimation or indirect comparison (e.g., lining up counters along each path; SMP 5).

STRATEGIES

- Children may draw paths from Audrey to the two outside doors.
- Children may guess at which path is shorter than the other.
- Children may visually compare the lengths of the paths to estimate which path is shorter.
- Children may make an indirect comparison of the lengths of the paths by lining up nonstandard units along the pathways (e.g., lima beans, teddy-bear counters, or linking cubes).
- Children may make an indirect comparison of the lengths of the paths by cutting yarn or string to the length of one or both pathways.

Misconceptions/Student Difficulties

- Children may struggle to conceptualize the floor-plan representation of Audrey's home and draw paths that pass through walls.
- Children may choose a shorter path based on which door Audrey is closest to, ignoring walls.
- If children use a nonstandard unit for indirect comparison, they will likely struggle to line up units end to end, without gaps or overlaps, thereby limiting their ability to compare accurately.
- Children may consider the number of rooms passed through as a measure of distance.

Launch

Review the expectations for fire drills in their school building. How would they exit the building? What path would they take, and where would they go? Examine an alternative path for exiting the building using a different door. Walk both of these routes with the children, and ask, "Which path do you think is the shorter route?" Have children share their ideas for which path is shorter. If they have particular ideas for how they made their comparisons (e.g., number of steps or number of rooms they had to pass through), explore these ideas. It may be helpful to revisit the paths, counting the number of steps for each or counting the number of rooms that they have to pass through. Also, highlight academic language that describes direction and their position in space such as *near to, through, straight ahead, right*, and *left*.

Ask, "Why is it important to have two different paths planned for getting out of the building?" Have children discuss their ideas, which will likely include the possibility of a fire or another dangerous event blocking one path. Tell the children that it is important for them to know two ways to get out of their own homes in case of an emergency for the same reasons.

Present the task to the students by reading it aloud. Display a visual of the floor plan for Audrey's home. Ask the children, "What do you think we are looking at here?" Ask them to share their ideas. Then show them a sketch of either the floor plan of their classroom or school space or that of a dollhouse they play with in school. Have students make comparisons between what they know about their space and the floor-plan image or what they see when they look down on the dollhouse and the floor plan of that space. Discuss representations of walls (solid lines), doors within the building (open gaps between solid lines), and doors to exit the building (rectangles marked *door*). If possible, draw the two paths that were identified earlier on the floor plan of the children's space.

Tell the children that they will be given a map of Audrey's home with a stick figure representing Audrey in one of the rooms. They are to identify two paths that Audrey could take to get out of her house in case of an emergency. Encourage them to use different colors to draw the paths. Also ask them to try to determine which path is shorter so Audrey knows which one to take in case of an emergency. Ask children to turn to a classmate and explain to them what they are going to do.

EXPLORE

Have children work either independently or in pairs with a map of Audrey's home. Provide colored pencils or markers for them to mark her two different paths. As children work, circulate throughout the room and ask the following questions to assess their understanding:

- Where should Audrey walk in case of an emergency? Can you show me the two different paths with your finger?
- Can you describe how Audrey should walk through her home? (Attend to academic language highlighting Audrey's direction or position in space.)
- Do these paths get Audrey out of her home in different ways? How do you know?
- Which path do you think is shorter?
- Why do you think this path is shorter?
- How many rooms does Audrey need to pass through for this path? What about the other path?
- Which path do you think Audrey should take if there is something dangerous in the (kitchen, parents' bedroom, living room)? Why?

Look for evidence in children's responses that they understand that the path they have drawn is a representation of where Audrey will walk from the location of her stick figure to get out of the house.

If children are finished with one set of paths and have decided which path is shorter, ask them to find two paths from a different room. Have additional floor plans available for this possibility.

Children may also be interested in extending this task to their own home. They may attempt to make a floor plan of their house and identify paths they may take to get out. Be aware that creating their own floor plans will be very challenging for them. They may make different spaces for rooms with connectors (e.g., hallways that do not actually exist in their homes). They may also struggle with organizing the different rooms spatially with a bird's-eye view. Encourage them to talk about their diagrams and how they would go through different rooms to get out of their homes rather than expect accuracy from their diagrams.

SUMMARIZE

Ask children to come to a meeting space to discuss the different ways that Audrey could get out of her house. Display children's work for different floor plans together, beginning with the kitchen. Ask one child to explain one of the paths from his or her work; ask another child to explain another path. Ask children who didn't find paths for Audrey's exit from the kitchen to describe what Audrey is doing on each of these paths.

Next, ask all the children to estimate which path is shorter. This may be straightforward for the paths from the kitchen because there is a door that allows exit from the kitchen directly. Have several students articulate their thinking, and ask if the class agrees that one particular path is shorter. If there are students who used indirect comparison to compare the two paths, have them share their strategies.

Repeat these questions for the other three locations of the house: bathroom, living room, and Audrey's room. Focus justification and discussion on the comparison of length of the two paths. Ask students to share and demonstrate strategies for comparing the lengths. Help students to articulate comparative sentences, such as, "The path through the kitchen looks shorter than the path through the front door." Highlight important language involving comparison and children's location in space, in this case, *shorter than* and *through*.

Finally, reiterate the importance of knowing multiple exit paths from their homes. Ask children to explore paths out of their own homes and to talk with their parents or guardians about what to do in the case of an emergency. Note that children may be encouraged to consider windows as potential exits.

DIFFERENTIATION

- If children struggle with understanding the connection between the floor plan and an actual home (e.g., lines are walls), create a floor plan of the children's classroom and have them map paths that will get them from different areas to the outside of the building.

- Alternatively, ask parents ahead of time to sketch a floor plan of their own homes. Children can then identify different paths out from various rooms in their own home.

- For an additional challenge, have students sketch floor plans of their own homes or of their prekindergarten space and identify exit paths from each room.

COMPARING PUMPKINS

Cade and Elias went to the pumpkin patch and picked out pumpkins. On the ride home they got into an argument over whose pumpkin was bigger. How can Cade and Elias tell whose pumpkin is bigger?

CCSSM STANDARD FOR MATHEMATICAL PRACTICE

Practice 3: Construct viable arguments and critique the reasoning of others.

CCSSM STANDARDS FOR MATHEMATICAL CONTENT

K.MD.A.1: Describe measurable attributes of objects, such as length or weight. Describe several measurable attributes of a single object.

K.MD.A.2: Directly compare two objects with a measurable attribute in common, to see which object has "more of" or "less of" the attribute, and describe the difference.

PROBLEM DISCUSSION

"Preschoolers can be guided to learn important measurement concepts if provided appropriate measurement experiences" (Fuson, Clements, and Beckmann 2010, p. 60). The goal of "Comparing Pumpkins" is to have students define and share ideas about which attributes are measurable, not necessarily on the precision of the measurements. Small groups discuss and explore measurable attributes of actual pumpkins (K.MD.A.1). Through hands-on experimentations, students investigate questions related to measurable attributes, such as how wide, how tall, how heavy, how round, and so forth. Students use these ideas to decide which measurable attribute is a reasonable one to use for comparing two pumpkins.

Using standard or nonstandard units of measurement, students determine which pumpkin has "more of" or "less of" the attribute (K.MD.A.2). Comparing the length of two objects begins with direct comparisons of the two objects and is followed by indirect comparison in which a third object is used (Clements and Sarama 2009). Direct comparison requires students to conserve length (i.e., when an object is moved, its length does not change). Indirect comparison requires students to employ transitive reasoning to use a third object to compare the lengths of two other objects. Throughout this task, students work in groups or with partners to choose attributes that can be measured, justify their choices, and explain how they plan to measure these attributes (SMP 3).

STRATEGIES

- Students may directly compare the pumpkins without using units to measure the attribute.
- Students may use the same units to measure all attributes.
- Students may use different units to measure the same attribute.

- Students may use units to measure both pumpkins, and then directly compare those lengths to determine which has more of that attribute. For example, they may use linking cubes to measure the height of each pumpkin, resulting in two cube towers, and directly compare those towers.
- Students may use units to measure both pumpkins, keeping track of the count for each pumpkin, and compare the final counts to determine which has more of that attribute.

Misconceptions/Student Difficulties

- Students may focus on nonmeasureable attributes such as color, texture, and so forth.
- Students may choose units that are not easy to lay end to end. For example, they may choose teddy-bear counters to measure the height of the pumpkin.
- Students may not see the need to measure the same attribute for both pumpkins using the same unit. For example, to measure height, they use teddy-bear counters for one pumpkin and paper clips for the other.

Launch

Ask students if they have ever gone to a pumpkin patch, and have them describe what they saw. This discussion may lead students to describe "big" and "little" pumpkins. As students describe the pumpkins, keep track of the words they use, such as *tall, short, heavy, wide, skinny, small, large, fat,* and so on. Ask students to use their body to show a pumpkin like each of the attributes in the list. For example, to show a skinny pumpkin, students may place their arms at their sides or position their hands to show a narrow opening between them.

Place a pumpkin for all students to see. Ask students which measuring tool in the classroom would be best to measure how tall the pumpkin is. Choose one of the tools suggested, hold up one of the units, and ask students to predict how many units tall the pumpkin is. Ask a student to come up and use the units to measure the pumpkin. Ask students if they think there is another way to measure how tall the pumpkin is. If so, have another student show how he or she would measure the pumpkin.

Ask the following questions to check for understanding:

- What do you notice about how (student name) used the (units) to measure the pumpkin?
- Why do you think (student name) measured the pumpkin this way?
- Why do you think (student name) and (student name) came up with different measurements?

Explore

Read the task to students and give each small group two pumpkins of different shapes and sizes. Ask students to take turns telling their group what they think Cade and Elias should measure to determine which pumpkin is bigger.

Ask these questions to check for understanding:

- Why do you think that is a good way to compare the pumpkins?
- How are the pumpkins the same? How are they different?
- How would you measure that (attribute)?
- Which pumpkin do you think is "more" or "less"?

Have students share their group's ideas about what to measure.

Tell students they can use any classroom tools to measure the attributes they discussed, including linking cubes, string, scale, pencils, paper clips, and so on. Allow students to use the tools to measure the attributes their group decided were good ways to measure the pumpkins.

Ask the following questions to check for understanding:

- What are you measuring?
- Why did you use (units) to measure the pumpkin?
- How many of the (units) do you predict you will need to find your answer?
- Is there another way you could use (units) to measure (how tall, how skinny, etc.)?
- How did you know which one was (taller, skinnier, fatter, etc.)?

SUMMARIZE

Ask students to pick the attribute they think Cade and Elias should use to determine which pumpkin is bigger. Have students draw a picture for Cade and Elias showing their group's pumpkins and how they measured the pumpkins to determine which was bigger.

Have students present their pictures to the class. As they share, record the attribute and the units used to measure the pumpkins. Make note of when the same attribute was measured using different units, and ask students which unit they think would be easier to use to measure that attribute.

DIFFERENTIATION

- To accommodate struggling students, assign them two attributes to measure.
- To accommodate struggling students, allow them to directly compare the pumpkins using visual estimates to determine which has more or less of a given attribute.
- To extend this task, ask questions like the following:
  - o How many more or fewer paper clips tall is this pumpkin?
  - o Which pumpkin is the tallest pumpkin in the room? Shortest? Skinniest? Heaviest?
- To extend this task, ask various students to arrange all of the pumpkins in order of height, width, weight, and so forth.

PUMPKINS

Mrs. Weaver is going to bring 8 pumpkins to school to decorate her classroom. Some are small and some are large. How many of each size could Mrs. Weaver bring to school? Use pictures, words, and numbers to show your thinking.

CCSSM STANDARD FOR MATHEMATICAL PRACTICE

Practice 8: Look for and express regularity in repeated reasoning.

CCSSM STANDARDS FOR MATHEMATICAL CONTENT

K.OA.A.3: Decompose numbers less than or equal to 10 into pairs in more than one way, e.g., by using objects or drawings, and record each decomposition by a drawing or equation (e.g., 5 = 2 + 3 and 5 = 4 + 1).

K.CC.B.5: Count to answer "how many?" questions about as many as 20 things arranged in a line, a rectangular array, or a circle, or as many as 10 things in a scattered configuration; given a number from 1–20, count out that many objects.

K.CC.C.6: Identify whether the number of objects in one group is greater than, less than, or equal to the number of objects in another group, e.g., by using matching and counting strategies.

PROBLEM DISCUSSION

This problem focuses on part-part-whole relationships, an important concept for the primary years. The whole is the quantity of pumpkins that Mrs. Weaver brings to school. The two parts are the subsets of the whole quantity, in this case, the number of small pumpkins and the number of large pumpkins. This problem is classified as a put-together/take-apart problem, both addends unknown (K.OA.A.3). Because both addends are unknown, there are multiple answers to this problem that the students can justify with objects or drawings (e.g., three small pumpkins and five large pumpkins) and equations (e.g., 3 + 5 = 8).

Eight can be decomposed in multiple ways: 0 + 8, 1 + 7, 2 + 6, 3 + 5, 4 + 4, 5 + 3, 6 + 2, 7 + 1, and 8 + 0. Although addends are reversible (3 + 5 is the same as 5 + 3), these are different answers in relation to the context of the problem. That is, three small pumpkins and five large pumpkins is a solution different from five small pumpkins and three large pumpkins. The context also suggests that there is at least one of each size pumpkin. Therefore, solutions involving zero small or large pumpkins may not be viewed as viable solutions, but students may discuss whether or not these solutions should be included.

This problem incorporates content standards related to the counting and cardinality domain. Students must accurately count up to eight items (K.CC.B.5), and may quickly recognize the number associated with a collection of objects without counting one by one (a concept referred to as *subitizing*). The discussion of the problem will also incorporate comparison concepts in which the quantities of small and large pumpkins can be identified as *greater than, less than,* or *equal to* (K.CC.C.6).

Together, the class can generate a table of possible solutions. Strategic ordering of these solutions can help students examine gaps where possible solutions have been missed. If the class realizes that there is no solution with five small pumpkins, for example, they are faced with a put-together/take-apart problem with one addend unknown. The structure of the table can be used to find the missing addend (SMP 8).

Number of Small Pumpkins	Number of Large Pumpkins	Picture	Equation
1	7		1 + 7 = 8
2	6		2 + 6 = 8
3	5		3 + 5 = 8
4	4		4 + 4 = 8
5	3		5 + 3 = 8
6	2		6 + 2 = 8
7	1		7 + 1 = 8

STRATEGIES

- Students may directly model the problem using blocks, pumpkin cutouts, or by drawing pictures to represent the situation. Students may also use a counting-on or counting-down strategy.
- A common representation is a fair-shares approach, using four small and four large pumpkins.
- Students may simply write a number pair such as 4 and 4.
- Students may list more than one number pair for 8 and may include equations to show their number pairs add to 8.
- Students may list all the number pairs for 8 or equations that result in 8.

MISCONCEPTIONS/STUDENT DIFFICULTIES

- If students are using objects or drawing pictures, they may miscount the total number of pumpkins.
- If students are using a counting-on or counting-down strategy, they may make a counting error; for example, there are six small pumpkins and the student counts up "six, seven, eight" and says they need "three large pumpkins."

LAUNCH

Begin by asking students how many of them decorate their house with pumpkins to celebrate fall. The teacher may choose to show pictures of the many varieties of pumpkins.

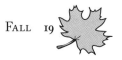

To prepare students for the size aspect of this task, ask the following:

- Are all pumpkins the same size?
- What sizes can they be?

Students can also be asked to use their arms to show the size of a small pumpkin and a large pumpkin. Read the task aloud to the students. A large, sealed box may be used to prompt students' thinking about an unknown quantity of small and large pumpkins. Emphasize that there are eight pumpkins in the box.

EXPLORE

Students work in pairs or groups of three to identify one possible answer to the problem. Multiple tools for representation should be provided. These may include Unifix cubes of two different colors, colored chips, and cutouts of large and small pumpkins.

As students work together, circulate throughout the room, prompting students to attend to pictures, words, and numbers in their solution. For example, a group might provide one picture of three small pumpkins and five large pumpkins, label their solution as "3 small and 5 large," and write an expression or an equation, 3 + 5 or 3 + 5 = 8.

Ask these questions to check for understanding:

- How do you know that you have eight pumpkins all together?
- How many small pumpkins do you have? How do you know?
- How many large pumpkins do you have? How do you know?
- Is the number of small pumpkins greater than, less than, or equal to the number of large pumpkins?

For students who are struggling to find a combination of small and large pumpkins that totals to eight, provide the eight-frame so students can use each square to place a manipulative or picture of a pumpkin.

After students have identified one combination of small and large pumpkins, have them create a poster that is a picture representation of the combination and write the quantity of each size as well as an expression or equation. If students are struggling with writing words at this age, provide handouts with the phrases " _____ small pumpkins" and " _____ large pumpkins" so they can fill in the appropriate numerals. If students are not prepared for writing expressions and equations, this can be developed during the mathematical discussion.

Finally, for students who have quickly identified one combination of small and large pumpkins and have finished their poster, challenge them to find other combinations that may work. Additional prompts might include the following:

- Can you find a combination where the number of small and large pumpkins is the same?

• Is your number of small pumpkins greater than or less than your number of large pumpkins? Can you find a combination where it's the opposite of what you have right now?

SUMMARIZE

Before the lesson, prepare a table (see page 19) to fill in the solutions that students find for the possible number of small and large pumpkins. Students' sharing of solutions may be purposefully sequenced such that the solutions begin with one small pumpkin and work sequentially toward seven small pumpkins. Student groups should discuss their solution and explain how they know there are eight pumpkins total. Ask groups as needed, "How does your picture show your combination of small and large pumpkins?" For the first solution, fill in the table as follows: the numeral 1 in the first column and 7 in the second column. The students' pictures for this solution can be reproduced in the third column or may be cut out from the poster and added to the column. If other student groups have generated the same solution, they should share their picture and strategy for solving the problem. Different pictures and representations can be added to the third column.

Then, demonstrate how the equation for this combination ($1 + 7 = 8$) can be written. (If students are able to write equations themselves, then this should be part of their presentation.) Ask what each of the values in the equation represents according to the problem's context; for example, the 1 represents the number of small pumpkins. Also, probe students about why a plus symbol is used and what the equals sign signifies in the equation.

Other combinations should be presented in order, filling in the table for each combination. As the process progresses, ask students about similarities in their solution strategies and picture representations. Also, pose questions like the following to students to increase their involvement in filling in the table:

• (Students) drew three small pumpkins and five large pumpkins. Does anyone have any idea of where I should put the three and the five in the table?
• How are the numbers in this row similar to (or different from) the numbers in this other row?

The students should identify the quantities that go in each of the first two columns, and some may be comfortable articulating equations for the combinations.

Throughout the discussion, attend to counting strategies and accuracy as well as comparisons of greater than, less than, and equal to. The discussion may also provide opportunities for analysis beyond the singular solutions, such as the following:

Attention to patterns. Students may notice that the values in the first column increase by one while the values in the second column decrease by one. Discuss why this is occurring and why it makes sense according to the context of the problem.

Missing combinations. There may be one or more combinations missing from the potential solutions in the table. Leave an empty row for these gaps, and ask students how the pattern might help them figure out what is missing. Or provide the absent quantity for small pumpkins and have them explore finding the unknown addend.

Zero. Students may wonder whether or not it is possible to have zero small or zero large pumpkins. Students should share their reasoning and justification around their opinions. If desired, explore the combinations for zero small pumpkins and zero large pumpkins.

All possible solutions. Students may wonder if all of the possible solutions have been found. Ask, "Do you think we have them all? How do we know?" Push thinking beyond seeing that all of the rows of the table are filled to thinking about the patterns happening in each column. For example, "Are there any possibilities for the number of small pumpkins that we have missed? How do you know?"

DIFFERENTIATION

- The total number of pumpkins can be adjusted to meet students' needs. Five may be a more appropriate quantity for some students to work with. Nine or ten total pumpkins may provide extensions for others.

- Some students may find combinations that total eight fairly quickly and easily. Challenge these students by asking whether or not they have found all of the possible combinations. How do they know?

- Another extension may involve three sizes of pumpkins: small, medium, and large. Challenge students to find one or more combinations of these three sizes that could comprise the eight total pumpkins: "What if Mrs. Weaver had three sizes of pumpkins—small, medium, and large? How many of each size could she have brought to school?"

FIVE LUCKY TURKEYS

On Thanksgiving Day, Carla saw five very lucky wild turkeys cross the road. How many legs on those turkeys did Carla see? Show your thinking.

CCSSM STANDARD FOR MATHEMATICAL PRACTICE

Practice 1: Make sense of problems and persevere in solving them.

CCSSM STANDARD FOR MATHEMATICAL CONTENT

K.CC.B.5: Count to answer "how many?" questions about as many as 20 things arranged in a line, a rectangular array, or a circle, or as many as 10 things in a scattered configuration; given a number from 1–20, count out that many objects.

PROBLEM DISCUSSION

In "Five Lucky Turkeys," students count the total number of legs on five turkeys who have survived another Thanksgiving Day. Because each turkey has two legs, students explore making ten by adding 5 twos: 2 + 2 + 2 + 2 + 2 = 10. They may not see this as addition but rather as counting, once the problem has been represented with a drawing or manipulatives (K.CC.B.5).

Students have the opportunity to make sense of the problem by drawing a picture or representing the turkeys' legs with manipulatives (SMP 1). They can then use their representation to count the total number of legs. Teachers may choose to connect this to a ten-frame by arranging turkey legs as in the following representation in which each shade indicates the legs of one turkey. This ten-frame representation may challenge students because it is filled by columns rather than by rows, the more common practice. Thus, they are seeing a ten-frame filled by 5 twos as opposed to 2 fives.

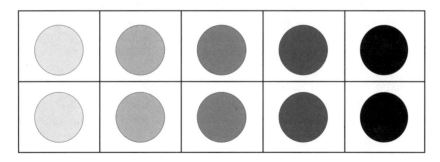

This task can be expanded to different numbers of turkeys and the relationship between the number of turkeys and the number of legs. (The number of turkey legs is double the number of turkeys.) The task could be modified at the outset by providing each pair of students a different number of turkeys rather than having them all process the solution for five turkeys.

Strategies

- Students may draw five turkeys, each with two legs, and use the drawing to count the total number of legs.
- Students may use a manipulative to represent the legs on each turkey. These manipulatives may be uniform in color, or students may differentiate between the turkeys by using a different color for each turkey.
- Students may use tally marks to represent each turkey's legs and count the total number of marks.
- Students may recognize that there are two legs on each turkey and skip-count by twos five times.

Misconceptions/Student Difficulties

- Students may think that there should be four legs on each turkey.
- Students may miscount the total number of legs in their representation because of errors with the rote counting sequence or one-to-one correspondence.
- Students may make errors with the skip counting by twos sequence. Students may also struggle with keeping track of the number of turkeys when skip-counting and land on the incorrect quantity.

Launch

Ask students how many of them are looking forward to Thanksgiving dinner. Have them identify different foods that are typically shared at a Thanksgiving dinner. Write their ideas down; for each item, ask them how many like that particular food item. Ask the class, "What type of meat is usually served at Thanksgiving dinner?" Although some of them may have meats other than turkey, discuss how turkey has historically been the centerpiece of the holiday's feast.

Read the task aloud to students. Ask them why the task is titled "Five Lucky Turkeys." This might be a good occasion to discuss the presidential pardon of a turkey at each Thanksgiving. Direct students to imagine five turkeys crossing the road and ask, "What does this look like in your mind?" Make sure that students know how many legs a turkey has. This may be information that many students do not know.

If this is a first experience for students in problem solving, you may discuss some strategies for working out a solution. Ask students, "Do you have any ideas about how you might solve this problem?" Have students share their thoughts; suggest drawing a picture or using manipulatives to show the turkeys' legs if these methods do not surface naturally.

Explore

Students work in pairs to solve this problem. Provide multiple materials for each pair: Unifix cubes and other manipulatives, drawing paper, and writing utensils. Let each pair of students make sense of the problem and pursue their own problem-solving strategy.

Pose questions like the following to each pair of students to assess their understanding of the problem and how their strategy matches the context of the problem:

- Can you tell me about the picture you have drawn?
- How many turkeys have you drawn? Can you show me the legs on the turkeys you have drawn?
- How are you planning to use your picture to answer the question?
- Can you tell me about the manipulatives you're using? How does this relate to the problem about the five turkeys?
- Why have you chosen to use different colors?
- How are you planning to use these tools to answer the question?
- How did you get the answer of ten (or another quantity) turkey legs? Can you tell me how you counted?
- Is there a way you can record your skip-counting by writing numbers? What do you think you might write?

It may be tempting to correct incorrect answers at this point, but try to guide students to realize a mistake through questioning. Errors with counting might be corrected by asking the pair of students to count the quantity together. If there is a misrepresentation of the problem, attempt to use questions linking their representation to the problem so they can identify the error. Consider letting incorrect answers proceed to the Summarize section, where the groups can discuss the importance of understanding and representing a problem, as well as the many skills that are involved with accurate counting.

If pairs are done quickly, provide another number of turkeys for which they need to solve the problem. Give each pair a different number from one through ten. Tell them to prepare to share their answers for this second problem as well.

Summarize

Display students' work for the "Five Lucky Turkeys" problem throughout the classroom. Ask students to do a gallery walk, paying attention to the different ways of solving the problem and noticing any similarities or differences with their own methods or between methods.

When the class has finished looking at all of the students' work, ask the following questions:

- How many groups chose to draw a picture to represent the problem?
- What was similar about their drawings? What was different?
- Did everyone get the same answer?

Ask a student to demonstrate how to get to the answer of ten turkey legs by counting the legs on a drawing. If there are pairs of students that did not get ten turkey legs, ask them to demonstrate how they counted or to show their drawing that gave them a different answer.

Modify the questions above for other strategies, such as using a manipulative to represent the turkeys and their legs or counting by twos. For students who used different representations for the turkeys and their legs, ask them to make connections between their representation and the others, including connections between the manipulatives and the drawings. For groups that counted by twos to find the answer, ask them to demonstrate how they arrived at ten turkey legs and how they knew when to stop skip counting.

Finally, if students have pursued the number of legs for other quantities of turkeys, ask them to share their answers. Make a two-column table of the results.

Number of Turkeys	Number of Legs
1	2
2	4
3	6
4	8
5	10
6	12
7	14
8	16
9	18
10	20

Ask students the following questions about the table of values:

- Does anyone see a pattern in the table? What do you notice?
- How many turkey legs would there be for eight turkeys? Where do you see that answer in the table?
- If there is a missing value, ask if anyone can predict how many turkey legs there would be for (missing number)turkeys.
- Can anyone tell me how many turkeys there would be if Carla had counted twelve legs on turkeys crossing the road?

DIFFERENTIATION

- For students who struggle with the task, provide pictures of turkeys. Have them count out five turkeys from a larger set.
- Consider reducing the number of turkeys for students who struggle to count to ten.
- Consider increasing the number of turkeys for students who find an answer quickly.
- Ask students a reverse question: How many turkeys are there if Carla sees twelve legs on the turkeys crossing the road?
- Ask students how many beaks, wings, or toes there were on the turkeys.
- Ask students how the answer might be different if there were a different kind of animal crossing the road.

APPLES

An apple market gets apples in large crates. The market likes to sell apples in bags that hold 10 apples.

(a) Can you help the market find the total number of apples in a crate?

(b) How many bags will you need for your apples and how many apples are left over?

(c) After you take away the bad apples, how many apples are left in your crate? How many bags will the market need for your crate?

CCSSM Standard for Mathematical Practice

Practice 7: Look for and make use of structure.

CCSSM Standards for Mathematical Content

1.NBT.B.2: Understand that the two digits of a two-digit number represent amounts of tens and ones. Understand the following as special cases:

- 10 can be thought of as a bundle of ten ones—called a "ten."
- The numbers 10, 20, 30, 40, 50, 60, 70, 80, 90 refer to one, two, three, four, five, six, seven, eight, or nine tens (and 0 ones).

1.NBT.C.6: Subtract multiples of 10 in the range 10–90 from multiples of 10 in the range 10–90 (positive or zero differences), using concrete models or drawings and strategies based on place value, properties of operations, and/or the relationship between addition and subtraction; relate the strategy to a written method and explain the reasoning used.

Problem Discussion

This problem allows students to practice counting between 40 and 100 objects in a strategic manner. Students may do this by grouping items into twos, fives, or tens and skip counting to find a total. To understand and work flexibly with the base-ten number system, students "need ample opportunities to bundle or group objects by tens and then count by tens" (Dougherty et al. 2010, p. 37). The context of the problem motivates students to place objects into "bundles" of ten and skip-count to find a total number of apples (1.NBT.B.2).

Students are given piles of 40–99 manipulatives, which represent their crate of apples. Once students create bundles of tens, they will need to "transition from viewing 'ten' as simply the accumulation of 10 ones to seeing it both as 10 ones and as 1 ten" (NCTM 2000, p. 33) to find out how many bags are needed. In the second part of this task students will be provided with a "bad apples" slip indicating the number of bad apples in their crates. This additional information requires students to subtract multiples of 10 from their total number of apples (1.NBT.C.6). Students will further examine the base-ten number system to realize that, for example, 20 is two groups of ten, or two bags of apples with no leftover apples (SMP 7).

Strategies

- Students may count all the apples one by one and use place-value concepts to decompose the two-digit number into groups of tens and ones. For example, if a student counts 68 apples, he says, "I have 60 and 8 which is 6 bags of 10 and 8 leftover apples."

- Students may separate apples into groups of twos, fives, or tens and skip-count to find the total number of apples, adding the leftovers one at a time. For example, if a student has seven groups of 10 with 3 left over she may count, "10, 20, 30, 40, 50, 60, 70, 71, 72, 73."

- Students may remove the number of apples on the bad apple slip one by one and recount all to find the new total number of apples.

- Students may remove the number of bad apples by skip-counting by twos, fives, or tens. For example, if they have 20 bad apples to remove, they may take away 2 apples at a time until they reach 20. Then students will recount by twos, fives, or tens to find the new total number of apples.

- Students may notice that the number of bad apples can be thought of in terms of bags with no leftover apples and remove whole bags of apples to find the new total number of apples.

Misconceptions/Student Difficulties

- Students miscount the number of apples in their shipment, which results in the number of bags and leftovers not correlating with their initial count.

- Students fail to recognize that a group of ten also represents 10 ones without needing to recount each time.

- If students are using a counting-on strategy, they may have a counting error such as counting on from six apples by counting "six, seven, eight, nine, ten" and saying they need "five more apples to make ten."

- Students may confuse the number of bags with the number of leftover apples.

Launch

Students work in pairs to solve this problem. Ask students if they go grocery shopping with a family member or friend. Ask them to talk to their partners about which fruits and vegetables are sold in bags, cartons, or by the bunch. After they discuss some ideas with their partners, ask them to share with the whole class. For example, they may mention apples, oranges, avocados, bananas, radishes, carrots, and so forth. Ask students to estimate how many of each fruit or vegetable comes in each bag, carton, or bundle. Ask them to record their thinking by drawing a picture of some of the items they have discussed with their partners. Have students present their drawings to the class.

If possible, bring in a bag of ten apples. Ask students to estimate how many apples are in the bag and to share their estimate and strategy with their partners; then have students present their estimates to the whole class. Next, have students count aloud with you as you remove the apples one by one.

Before class, prepare "crates of apples" for each pair of students, ranging from 40–99 manipulatives (e.g., linked cubes). Tell students that today they will be helping the market sort apples and determine how many bags they will need for the apple shipment.

EXPLORE

Give each pair of students a crate of apples. Students will also need paper and pencil to record their work. Read part (a) of the task to students and tell them they must first determine how many apples are in their shipment. Before students begin counting their apples, give them a couple of minutes to plan how they will count the apples. Ask these questions to check for understanding:

- How are you keeping track of the number of apples you have already counted?
- What is your plan for counting the apples? Why do you think this is a good plan?
- Why are you placing apples into groups of (number)? How do you know there are (number) apples in each group?

Once students have found the total number of apples in the shipment read part (b) of the task to the class and have students work with their partner to determine the number of bags of apples and the number of leftover apples in their shipment. Ask the following questions to check for understanding:

- How many apples are in each bag?
- Can you show me a bag of ten apples? Do you have enough apples to make another bag of ten apples?
- I see you have (number) bags and (number) leftover apples. How many apples are in the (number) bags? How many apples do you have altogether?

Next, inform students that they will now be inspectors for the market. Pairs should work with another pair, creating groups of four, and inspect each other's work to verify the counts are accurate. Then pairs should take turns sharing their total number of apples as well as how many bags and leftover apples they have. Students should also explain their strategies for determining these numbers. These may include making groups of ten and then counting the groups or counting by ones, twos, or fives; each time a ten is reached, a tally is marked.

Tell students that the market throws out bruised apples, and they will be given a report that shows how many of their apples need to be thrown out. Hand out one of the "bad apple" slips to each group.

Read part (c) of the task. Students may solve this task by removing the number of apples on the slip and recounting their new pile of apples. Others may notice that the number of bad apples can be thought of in terms of bags with no leftover apples and remove whole bags of apples. Ask these questions to check for understanding:

- Will you have more or fewer apples? How do you know?
- How many bags of apples would the bad apples fit into? How many leftover apples would there be?
- How many apples would you have if you had ten fewer apples?
- What do you notice about your original number of apples and the number of apples you have now?

SUMMARIZE

Ask students to share their strategies for removing the bad apples with the whole class. Ask a group that had to remove ten bad apples to state how many apples they had in their original shipment. Mark that number on the chart. Record the information in a table like the one below:

Total Apples in Shipment	Number of Bad Apples	New Total of Apples
56	10	46
43	10	33
72	10	62

After noting the numbers from the groups that needed to remove ten bad apples, ask students what they notice about the number of bags and leftovers when ten apples are removed. Focus on the structure of the number; for example, one group of ten apples is equivalent to one bag and the leftover apples (or the ones) remains the same. Also, concentrate on the academic language of *ten more than* and *ten less than*. It may be helpful to use sentence frames similar to those below using the numbers 46 and 36. Have students share their thinking and explain how they know it is *ten more than* or *ten less than*.

46 is 10 _____ _____ 36.
36 is 10 _____ _____ 46.

Repeat this process of displaying the numbers in a table for students who had twenty, thirty, and forty bad apples to remove, looking for patterns they see, and finally completing sentence frames for these groups who had different numbers of bad apples.

DIFFERENTIATION

- For students who struggle, reduce the size of their shipment.
- For students who struggle to keep track of groups of ten, provide them with ten-frames to keep track of their bags of ten apples.
- Allow students to use a hundreds chart to find the total number of apples before and after the bad apple slips are handed out.
- To extend this task, pose the following problems to students:
    - o The market is considering offering another size bag. How many apples do you think the market should sell in their new bag? How many bags of this size would you need for your shipment of apples?
    - o The market had a shipment of 76 apples. After the inspector went through the shipment and got rid of the bad ones, they now have 56 apples. How many bad apples were thrown out?
- To extend this task, ask students to work together to combine the leftover apples into bags of ten and find the total number of bags the market needs for all the apples.

Harvest Celebration

Your help is needed to plan the Fall Harvest Celebration.

(a) Planners want the gym to be partitioned into two equal sections, one for eating dinner and the other for playing games. How do you think the planners should partition the gym?

(b) The planners have decided to divide the eating section into two equal sections: one for adults and one for children. They want to do the same for the games section. How do you think the planners should partition the gym?

CCSSM Standard for Mathematical Practice

Practice 4: Model with mathematics.

CCSSM Standard for Mathematical Content

1.G.A.3: Partition circles and rectangles into two and four equal shares, describe the shares using the words *halves, fourths*, and *quarters*, and use the phrases *half of, fourth of,* and *quarter of.* Describe the whole as *two of,* or *four of the shares.* Understand for these examples that decomposing into more equal shares creates smaller shares.

Problem Discussion

"To understand fractions, students must be able to partition a whole into equal portions and understand how the portions are related to the whole" (Battista 2012, p. 2). This task focuses on the development of fraction knowledge as students are asked to partition a rectangular area into two and four equal shares and to describe the shares using words like *halves* (*half of*), *fourths* (*fourth of*), and *quarters* (*quarter of*) (1.G.A.3). Students also explore the notion that when a shape is partitioned into additional equal-size shares, those shares become smaller.

Students investigate multiple ways to partition a rectangle, that is, the gym, into two and four equal portions for the harvest celebration, and then determine which partitions result in the most practical use of the space in the gymnasium (SMP 4). For example, students may realize that partitioning the rectangle along the diagonals will result in very small areas near the intersection of the diagonal and the vertices of the rectangle; however, dividing the shape in half along a line of symmetry does not result in these small areas.

Strategies

- Students may fold their papers vertically and horizontally to make equal shares.
- Students may draw vertical and horizontal lines to make equal-size shares.
- Students may use diagonals or oblique lines to make equal shares.
- Students may cut out the shares to verify that they are equal in size.

Misconceptions/Student Difficulties

- Students may partition the gym into two or four equal sections, but not understand how each section relates to the whole. For example, they may not be able to say that one of the two sections is *half of the whole*.
- Students may be unable to grapple with the diagonal or oblique lines, especially for the rectangle, because the diagonal is not a line of symmetry.
- Students may ignore the need for the shares to be equal in size and simply attend to the number of pieces needed.

Launch

Ask students if they know what people are celebrating during a harvest celebration. Discuss what happens during a harvest and which types of food are harvested in their area. Are these foods harvested in the fall? Discuss foods that are harvested in the fall, such as corn, beans, wheat, oats, barley, apples, carrots, cabbage, and so forth. Ask students if they have ever been to a harvest celebration. If they have, ask them where the celebration occurred and to describe activities that occurred during the celebration.

Explore

Give students rectangular sheets of paper and tell them that to celebrate the fall harvest, a large community dinner is being planned, and it will be held in the school gym. The planners have asked the class to help decide how the gym will be partitioned for the celebration. Read the task and part (a) to students. Let students work with a partner to find at least two different ways to partition the gym into two equal shares. Allow students to cut out shares to convince themselves that the shares are indeed equal in size. Ask these questions to check for understanding:

- How do you know the two shares are equal?
- Is there another way you can partition the gym into two equal shares?
- How much of the whole gym is this part (point at one half of the gym)? How do you know?

Have students present their partitioned rectangles to the class. Below are possible solutions. If students do not think of all three, challenge them to find another way. If they still cannot come up with all the solutions, display the one they are missing and ask if this rectangle is partitioned into equal shares and to justify their reasoning.

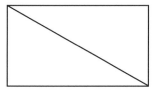 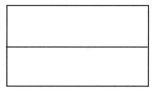 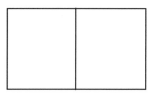

 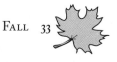

Ask the following questions to check for understanding:

- How much is each section of the whole gym?
- Are the two sections equal in size? How do you know?
- Do you think there are other ways to partition the gym into two equal sections? Explain.

Next, read part (b) of the task and have students determine how to partition the eating and games sections in half. Let students cut out shares to convince themselves that the shares are indeed equal in size. Ask these questions to check for understanding:

- How many equal shares is the gym divided into now?
- How much of the gym does this section (point to one of the four sections) represent?
- How much of the gym do these two sections (point to two of the four sections) represent?
- What do you notice about the size of these equal shares compared to the size of the equal shares from before? Are they larger or smaller?
- Do the sizes of the equal shares get larger or smaller the more times you divide them into equal parts?

SUMMARIZE

Have students share their solutions with the class. Display a drawing of each solution on the board. Below are examples of solutions that might be shared. Each time, ask students how they know their sections are the same size. Focus attention on the academic language, such as *half of, quarter of, fourth of,* and so forth. This can be done by pointing to shares and asking the student to describe the share in relation to the whole gym. Note that the two examples in the bottom row may require further discussion to verify that the shares are equal in area. The first one is easier to determine because the shares are the same shape. The second one requires cutting along the dashed line to create two right triangles. These two right triangles can be arranged to fill each of the other triangles.

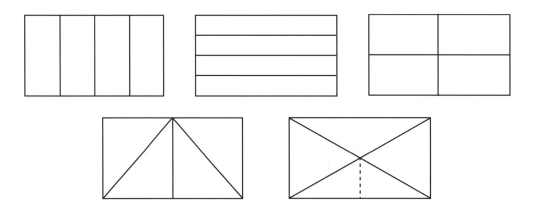

To conclude, ask students to examine each way to partition the gym into four equal shares and consider which of the possibilities would be best for the harvest celebration. Have students discuss their thoughts with a partner. Next, ask students to write a letter to the planner, including a picture of the partitioned gym and an explanation of why they think this is the best arrangement for the celebration.

DIFFERENTIATION

- For students struggling to partition the gym, provide them with rectangles representing the gym that are already partitioned into two and four parts. Have students sort the rectangles into those that have two or four equal shares and those that do not.

- To extend this task, ask students to draw pictures of foods they think will be eaten at the celebration and then divide those foods into halves and fourths (e.g., apple pie, pumpkin bars, ears of corn, etc.).

- To extend this task, lead a discussion about how to write the fractions for one-half and one-fourth.

- To extend this task, ask students, "If could could divide each of the four equal shares in half, how many equal shares would you have?"

Two Bales at a Time

On the Stanley farm, the bales of hay must be moved from the field to storage. Using a bale spear, Travis can lift and transport 1 or 2 bales of hay at a time. Moving 2 bales is challenging for Travis, and he wants to practice and get better. Travis's parents will let him choose which fields he wants to work. Which fields should Travis choose if he only wants to transport 2 bales of hay at a time? Explain your reasoning for each field of hay bales.

CCSSM Standards for Mathematical Practice

Practice 7: Look for and make use of structure.

Practice 8: Look for and express regularity in repeated reasoning.

CCSSM Standard for Mathematical Content

2.OA.C.3: Determine whether a group of objects (up to 20) has an odd or even number of members, e.g., by pairing objects or counting them by 2s; write an equation to express an even number as a sum of two equal addends.

Problem Discussion

In this situation, students are asked to sort fields based on whether they have an odd or an even number of hay bales (2.OA.C.3). Fifteen fields have been provided, each with a quantity of hay bales represented either numerically or pictorially. For each field, students can determine if two hay bales can be repeatedly removed until there are either none left over (even number) or one left over (odd number) (SMP 8). Students may be aware of the *even* and *odd* terminology; if not, the Summarize portion of this lesson is an opportunity to introduce them to these terms.

At the end of the problem, students will have sorted the fields into the two categories and justified their reasoning about one or more of the fields.

Fields with an Odd Number of Bales	Fields with an Even Number of Bales
Field A – 19	Field B – 14
Field C – 15	Field F – 22
Field D – 13	Field H – 34
Field E – 37	Field K – 46
Field G – 25	Field M – 20
Field I – 29	Field N – 38
Field J – 41	Field O – 40
Field L – 47	

In their justification, students ought to be able to demonstrate the process of pulling two manipulatives away repeatedly or of matching pairs of manipulatives or pictures until there are either none or one left over. For students who are reasoning more abstractly, they may be able to justify their reasoning by writing a number sentence. For example, they may represent 13 hay bales as $13 - 2 - 2 - 2 - 2 - 2 - 2 = 1$ left over or $13 = 2 + 2 + 2 + 2 + 2 + 2 + 1$.

Students may also recognize quantities as doubles or near doubles (e.g., $14 = 7 + 7$, a double ; $13 = 6 + 6 + 1$, a near double). Note, however, that the structure for the these equations does not directly correlate with the problem context because it recognizes an even number as two equal quantities rather than sets of 2. For example, 34 hay bales can be represented as two sets of 17, but seventeen sets of 2 are aligned with the context of the problem.

Ultimately, through this problem, students are examining the structure of a variety of values (SMP 7). They will start to recognize quantities that can be separated into pairs with or without one left over. They may connect this to skip counting by twos and recognize patterns that occur with this sequence of numbers. The goal for this lesson is not to generalize any sort of procedure for recognizing odd and even numbers (as determined by the last digit of the number). However, it is possible that if some sort of visual categorization of odd and even numbers is maintained over a period of time, with additional values added to this sort, students may recognize some similarities between the numbers in each category.

STRATEGIES

- With fields of hay bales that are represented pictorially, students may circle pairs of bales until no more pairs can be made.
- Students may represent the quantities of hay bales using a manipulative, such as Unifix cubes, and then repeatedly remove pairs of manipulatives to represent the two hay bales being moved at once.
- Students may represent the hay bales with a manipulative, such as Unifix cubes, and match two lines of the manipulative (i.e., line up pairs of manipulatives).
- Students may draw tally marks, circles, or some other picture to represent the hay bales, and then repeatedly cross out or circle pairs of pictures.
- Students may repeatedly subtract two from the quantity to see if one is left over.
- Students may try to identify whether or not a number is a *double* or *near double* quantity to determine if there will be one bale of hay left over.

MISCONCEPTIONS/STUDENT DIFFICULTIES

- Students may misunderstand the problem, choosing values of hay bales that are small to minimize Travis's work.
- Students may discard the remaining hay bale rather than see it as something that must be transported and, therefore, influencing Travis's choice.
- With crowded drawings, students may struggle to differentiate between bales of hay that have been moved as part of a pair and hay bales that remain.
- Students may make computational errors with addition or subtraction that influence the result.

Launch

Ask students if they have ever seen hay bales out in a field. Depending on students' experiences, they may or may not be familiar with farming hay, so be prepared to support the development of their understanding of the context by showing pictures of hay bales drying in a field or being transported.

Read the problem aloud to students. Ask one student to explain what is easy for Travis. Ask another student to describe what Travis finds challenging. Finally, ask students to turn to a neighbor to share what quantities of hay bales Travis should be looking for. They may articulate this as "Travis is looking for a number that we can make pairs of hay bales with none left over," or something similar to this idea. If multiple students seem confused, have a few of them relate their thoughts.

Finally, display six to ten field cards to the class and ask students to make predictions about the values. Again, have them turn to a neighbor and share their prediction about whether or not each is a quantity that Travis would want to transport. Ask a few students to report their predictions.

Explore

Assign students partners or groups of three. Tell each group that they will be investigating a few of the fields on the Stanley family farm. Looking at each field, they must decide whether or not it is a field that Travis should choose and to explain the reasoning for their choice. Provide each group with two to three field cards to investigate (mixing numerical and pictorial representations may be helpful) as well as manipulatives and other materials that might aid their investigation (e.g., linking cubes, color counters, and blank paper).

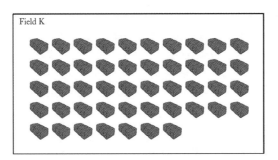

Allow groups some time to explore different ways to investigate the different quantities they have been given. After groups have begun to explore one of their fields, walk among the groups, asking these questions that may help them articulate their understanding:

- Why have you circled pairs of hay bales? What does that tell you?
- How many cubes do you have in this pile? Why did you count out this many?
- Why do you have cubes snapped together in pairs?
- What do these pairs tell you about Travis's work?

- I see that you have your hay bale drawings/tally marks grouped together in pairs. Why have you done that?
- How do you know that this is a field that Travis should ask to work on?
- How do you know that this is a field that Travis shouldn't ask to work on?
- Can you show me where you see a single hay bale to transport in your representation?
- Could you write a number sentence to show others your thinking?

If students are reasoning more abstractly through number sentences, ask how their reasoning connects to the context of the problem. Additionally, if students are thinking about quantities as doubles or near doubles, ask how the equal addends make sense in the context of the problem. They ought to be able to reason, for example, that in a field with fourteen hay bales (14 = 7 + 7), Travis would move pairs of hay bales seven times.

Groups use one recording sheet for each field they investigate, or they may justify their reasoning on white boards or chart paper. This is a valuable opportunity to have students justify their reasoning collaboratively and discuss various ways to represent their thinking for others. As students work, collect information about how each group has solved the problem. Record these strategies so various methods can be presented and discussed.

If groups have finished investigating their assigned fields, give them other cards to investigate. For students who are comfortable working with larger numbers, or who would benefit from this challenge, write larger quantities on the blank field cards (Fields P through Z).

SUMMARIZE

When students come together for the class discussion, call on groups to present their findings for a particular field. Based on observations from the Explore portion of the lesson, sequence students' work from the most concrete (e.g., circling pairs of hay bales or representing the hay bales with a manipulative and separating into pairs) to the most abstract (e.g., representing quantities of hay bales in an equation using doubles or near doubles). If possible, be sure that a variety of strategies are presented and that groups share their reasoning and justification for different fields. If groups came up with contradictory answers for specific fields, allow time for questions or comments. Another group may provide a counterargument for a particular field, as needed.

During or between presentations of strategies, ask questions that foster connections between strategies, such as the following examples:

- How was this group's strategy of making pairs of bales or cubes similar to what the other group did by removing pairs of cubes?
- Why does this drawing have pairs of pictures or tallies circled? How is this similar to what the other group did with the cubes?
- This group has subtracted two in an equation from the number of hay bales until they couldn't subtract any more. What does this strategy have in common with what we have seen with the cubes and drawings?

- How does this equation (e.g., 25 = 12 + 12 + 1) seem similar to what the other group did by matching up their cubes in two lines with one left over?
- How does this equation connect to the other strategies that have hay bales paired up?

These final questions will be challenging for students who may not see the connection to the context. If students were able to connect an equation using doubles or near doubles to the context of the problem, have them share their reasoning. However, it is likely there will be some lingering challenges for students who do not see the connection to the context.

After all the strategies that surfaced in the classroom have been described, ask students to explain their answers about the other fields and whether or not they should be fields that Travis chooses. Sort a set of the field cards into two categories: fields that Travis should choose and fields that he should not choose. If there are any questions or disagreements about any of the quantities, have students share their reasoning and critique each other's thinking until there is consensus.

Finally, explain the mathematical terminology of *odd* and *even*, describing the members of these categories. Ask students to turn to an elbow partner and discuss how they might describe odd numbers and even numbers. Ask students to present their descriptions and record them for later reference and/or refinement. If students have additional observations about the sets, provide some time for their discussion. However, leave these observations open as conjectures for further exploration. In future days and weeks, add numbers to these sets and let them speculate further about the conjectures.

Differentiation

- For students who struggle with counting larger quantities, offer cards with smaller values by using the blank field cards.
- If a class generally needs to focus on values 0–20, use the blank field cards to create values within this range.
- For students who are ready to be challenged with larger quantities, provide blank field cards with larger values written in.
- Challenge students by asking them which quantities Travis should choose if he wants to move hay bales three or four at a time.
- Challenge students by asking them to identify all values within a certain range (e.g., 0–30) that would be good choices for Travis. Can they find a pattern?

COUNTING BALLOTS

The polls have closed on Election Day, and Mr. and Mrs. Watson are counting ballots for the three candidates for mayor. Ten *loose* ballots can be grouped together with a rubber band to make a *bundle*. Ten of these bundles can be put into a *box*. When they finish counting all of the ballots, they have the following results.

	Boxes	Bundles	Loose Ballots
Candidate A	7	14	8
Candidate B	8	4	12
Candidate C	6	25	9

Can you determine how many votes each candidate for mayor has? Who has won the election? Explain how you know.

CCSSM Standards for Mathematical Practice

Practice 1: Make sense of problems and persevere in solving them.

Practice 5: Use appropriate tools strategically.

CCSSM Standards for Mathematical Content

2.NBT.A.1: Understand that the three digits of a three-digit number represent amounts of hundreds, tens, and ones; e.g., 706 equals 7 hundreds, 0 tens, and 6 ones.

2.NBT.A.4: Compare two three-digit numbers based on meanings of the hundreds, tens, and ones digits, using >, =, and < symbols to record the results of comparisons.

Problem Discussion

In "Counting Ballots," students are asked to consider total quantities when items are grouped by hundreds, tens, and ones (2.NBT.A.1). This is not as straightforward as simply combining hundreds, tens, and ones; rather, students need to think about regrouping ones and tens when their quantities are ten or greater. This happens in the case of each candidate:

- Candidate A's Votes: $700 + 140 + 8 = 700 + 100 + 40 + 8 = 800 + 40 + 8 = 848$
- Candidate B's Votes: $800 + 40 + 12 = 800 + 40 + 10 + 2 = 800 + 50 + 2 = 852$
- Candidate C's Votes: $600 + 250 + 9 = 600 + 200 + 50 + 9 = 800 + 50 + 9 = 859$

Students are also asked to compare the total number of votes for each candidate to determine the winner of the election (2.NBT.A.4). Despite Candidate C having the fewest number of boxes of votes at the end of counting ballots, Candidate C is the winner with 859 votes.

This task requires students to think about our base-ten place-value system. Loose ballots are the number of ones. Bundles are made by grouping ten loose ballots to represent a quantity of tens. Boxes are made by grouping ten bundles (10 tens) to represent a quantity of hundreds. In each candidate's representation, there are groupings that have not taken place. To determine the correct number of votes for the candidates, students need to think about how to combine these quantities of hundreds, tens, and ones appropriately. They will need to determine the value each number in the table represents, make sense of the amounts in relation to the context, and consider how these quantities might be used to determine the results of the election. They may need to reconsider their initial understanding of the way the ballots are grouped as they consider the number of loose ballots, bundles, and boxes for each candidate (SMP 1).

Students should be encouraged to use manipulatives to support their reasoning throughout this task (SMP 5). In particular, base-ten blocks would represent the boxes, bundles, and loose ballots with flat, long, and unit blocks, respectively. Students could actively group ten units (loose) and exchange that for one long (bundle), or group ten longs (bundles) and exchange that for one flat (box). Digiblocks or other alternatives may be used. Students should be provided access to the tools they are familiar with, understand, and can effectively use to represent the quantities in the problem.

STRATEGIES

- Students may use a groupable manipulative to represent the quantities in the problem. For example, they may "bundle" and "box" counters or toothpicks to represent the number of votes each candidate has received, according to the chart.
- Students may use a pregrouped manipulative to represent the quantities in the problem. For example, they may use base-ten blocks to represent the number of votes each candidate has received, according to the chart.
- Students may use the manipulatives to regroup into tens and hundreds when possible. Students may use the manipulatives (once all regrouping has occurred) to identify the number of hundreds, tens, and ones and determine the total number of votes for each candidate.
- Students may draw pictures to represent the quantities in the problem (e.g., tallies for loose, circles for bundles, and squares for boxes). Students may use these drawings to identify opportunities for exchange (ten loose for one bundle or ten bundles for one box).
- Students may identify the number of votes that is represented by each column and add these together (e.g., 700 + 140 + 8) using a variety of strategies based on place-value understanding.

MISCONCEPTIONS/STUDENT DIFFICULTIES

- Students may ignore the value of each of the quantities for the candidates' counts. For example, they may determine that Candidate A has 29 votes (7 + 14 + 8).

- Students may piece together the quantities without consideration of place value or the need to regroup. For example, they may determine that Candidate A has 7148 votes (7 boxes, 14 bundles, and 8 loose).
- Students may decide that Candidate B is the winner of the election because this candidate has the most boxes of votes.
- Students may struggle to regroup the 14 bundles, 25 bundles, or 12 loose ballots.
- Students may ignore quantities that do not "fit" into the number. For example, they may determine that Candidate A has 718 or 748 votes, disregarding the "extra" 4 tens for the former and the 10 tens for the latter. Or, they may determine that Candidate A has 808 votes by regrouping the 10 tens and ignoring the remaining 4 tens.
- Students may make computational errors when combining the quantities.

LAUNCH

Ask students if they know what Election Day is. Have students share their thoughts and understanding about Election Day. Their knowledge may be limited to presidential elections. Take some time to discuss the many offices that are determined by vote, and why this process is important to our democracy. This is also an opportunity to talk about the different ways that people vote around the country, including by mail or at local polling stations, electronically or with a paper ballot. Discuss how in most cases the winner of an election is decided by a simple majority vote. (The Electoral College makes the presidential election more complicated!)

Describe some local offices that are to be decided on Election Day. Highlight one office, and present the different candidates for this office. Indicate that the winner of this race will be the person who gets the most votes on Election Day.

Read the task aloud to students. Give the class time to process the different ways that ballots are being organized. It would be helpful to have several (ten or more) fake ballots to work with as students process loose ballots, bundles, and boxes. Be sure that everyone understands how many ballots are in a bundle of ballots (ten) and a box of ballots (10 tens, or 1 hundred).

Display the chart of votes earned by the three candidates. Ask students, "What do you notice about this chart?" Have them share any observations about the chart, including what they know about the quantities of loose, bundled, or boxed ballots for each candidate. Ask the students to make a prediction about who has won the election. Have students turn to a partner to explain their predictions and reasoning. Call on a few students to present their predictions to the class.

EXPLORE

Assign students to pairs or groups of three to work on this problem. Provide any materials that students have used previously to work on place-value concepts, such as base-ten blocks. Allow students some time to begin processing the different values that are provided for each candidate as they determine the number of votes each candidate has received in all.

As students work, circulate throughout the room, taking note of students' strategies for solving the problem. Pay particular attention to students' misconceptions in order to address these during the Summarize portion of the lesson. Ask the following questions to check for understanding:

- How did you find the total number of votes for Candidate A (B or C)?
- Can you explain to me what you did with the 14 bundles (or 12 loose or 25 bundles)?
- How did grouping the bundles together change the number of boxes for that candidate?
- How do you know that 25 bundles are equivalent to 250 loose ballots?
- How did you determine which candidate has won the election for mayor?

If students have demonstrated some of the misconceptions above, ask them to prove their answers using a tool or a manipulative.

If students struggle to get started with this problem, recommend that they use a manipulative from those provided. Ask, "How could you use these manipulatives to represent loose ballots, bundles, and boxes?" Be sure that the students see the correspondence between the manipulatives and place values: ones, tens, and hundreds.

Finally, ask students to create a poster showing their results. Recommend that their posters demonstrate their reasoning for each of the candidates.

Summarize

If students generally have similar solution strategies and answers, setting up a gallery walk may be appropriate way for them to share their results. However, if there is some discrepancy in who the students think has won, consider having groups defend each of their choices for the winner, starting with Candidate A, then Candidate B, and finally Candidate C.

As students discuss the strategies seen in the gallery walk or in students' presentations of strategies to the whole class, highlight the mathematical ideas of place value and exchange. Pay close attention to the 14 bundles of Candidate A, the 12 loose of Candidate B, and the 25 bundles of Candidate C, and what happens with these values as 10 loose are traded for a bundle and 10 bundles are swapped for a box. Discuss the implications of these exchanges on the digits in the hundreds, tens, and ones places of each number. If students have reasoned numerically about the total number of votes, highlight connections between the representations of the votes using manipulatives and the numerical calculations.

Also, take some time to discuss any misconceptions or challenges that surfaced in the Explore section of the lesson. This may involve revisiting the students' predictions from the Launch and why it may be surprising that the candidate that had the fewest number of boxes was actually the winner of the election.

 44 PROBLEM SOLVING IN ALL SEASONS

Finally, consider providing the students with another candidate's results. Candidate D could have 7 boxes, 15 bundles, and 1 loose ballot. Or for an additional challenge, Candidate D could have 6 boxes, 19 bundles, and 22 loose ballots. This latter option not only requires two regroupings, but the regrouping of the loose ballots provides enough bundles to force an additional regrouping of the bundles. Ask students if Candidate D would change the results of the election.

DIFFERENTIATION

- For students who are struggling to conceptualize numbers in the hundreds place, provide results that involve loose ballots and bundles and only regrouping of loose ballots.
- For students who struggle, consider reducing the number of candidates to Candidates A and B.
- To extend the task, ask students how they might change the results to get either Candidate A or Candidate B to win by a narrow margin.
- To challenge students, ask them to create a problem for other groups to solve by generating their own results for a close election for the school board.
- For students who reason quickly about ones, tens, and hundreds, consider giving them the aforementioned results for Candidate D during the Explore section of the lesson.
- For students who reason abstractly about ones, tens, and hundreds, consider expanding their task by including a fourth grouping for the candidates: trunks that are formed with ten boxes. Adjust the number of boxes for each candidate so students must consider the thousands place.

WINTER

Winter is the time when temperatures fall and, in many places, so does snow. From snow gear to sledding, cold weather provides a context for the majority of the tasks in this chapter. Additionally, the winter season includes the Super Bowl, Valentine's Day, and Presidents' Day—all wonderful themes for meaningful math activities.

The first task, "Kittens and Their Mittens," emphasizes academic language and requires prekindergarten students to identify patterns as well as to create one of their own. The second task for these learners focuses on counting and cardinality through the context of a "Sledding Race," in which students must order sleds from one to ten.

The two kindergarten tasks involve snow attire. "Ms. Frost's Scarves" focuses on decomposing and composing numbers less than or greater than ten. The other kindergarten task, "Snow Gear," is centered on students' use of positional language, such as *above, below, next to,* and *between* to place winter clothing into baskets.

First-grade students are encouraged to try a variety of strategies to find different ways to make 20 using multiple addends in "Sledding Fun," and in "Inches of Snowfall," these students are given clues using the vocabulary of *more than* or *less than* so they can create a bar graph related to monthly snowfall. In "Super Bowl Sunday" students use tools to order a player's three runs by their length.

The two second-grade tasks are related to the seasonal holidays of Presidents' Day and Valentine's Day. The first asks students to find different combinations of coins to make a given amount. Students are also encouraged to discuss the presidents whose faces are on each of the coins. In the last task of the chapter, second graders apply their understanding of repeated addition with equal groups to determine the number of valentines exchanged among five friends.

MATERIALS FOR EACH TASK, INCLUDING HANDOUTS, ARE AVAILABLE FOR DOWNLOADING AND PRINTING ON NCTM'S WEBSITE AT NCTM.ORG/MORE4U BY ENTERING THE ACCESS CODE ON THE TITLE PAGE OF THIS BOOK.

KITTENS AND THEIR MITTENS

Some kittens were outside playing on a snowy winter day. When they came in from the cold, they hung up their mittens to dry. The kittens argued about the pattern they should use when hanging up their mittens. Can you help the kittens decide? Use the mittens to create your own pattern.

CCSSM Standard for Mathematical Practice

Practice 8: Look for and express regularity in repeated reasoning.

Standard for Mathematical Content

According to NCTM's *Principles and Standards for School Mathematics* (2000) and *Curriculum Focal Points for Prekindergarten through Grade 8 Mathematics: A Quest for Coherence* (2006), patterning activities in prekindergarten through grade 2 are fundamental for the development of algebraic reasoning. "Patterns are a way for young students to recognize order and to organize their world and are important in all aspects of mathematics at this level" (NCTM 2000, p. 91). Specifically pre-K students should be able to "recognize and duplicate simple and sequential patterns" (NCTM 2006, p. 11).

Problem Discussion

A *repeating pattern* involves repetition of an identifiable core. Primary children usually begin pattern work with fairly simple patterns, such as AB, ABC, or ABB patterns. The letters represent elements while the sequence of letters represents the core that is repeated.

The elements within a repeating pattern can be unique, based on color, shape, orientation, and other variables. A simple AB pattern might have alternating Unifix cubes such as red, blue, red, blue, and so on. A more complex ABB pattern might consist of pattern blocks such as hexagon, square, square, hexagon, square, square, and so forth. Repeating patterns can also be composed of motions (e.g., clap, snap, snap, clap, snap, snap ...) or sounds (e.g., moo, quack, quack, moo, quack, quack ...).

Students see patterns in the world around them. Research shows that around three-fourths of children entering kindergarten can copy a repeated pattern (Clements and Sarama 2007). However, less than one-third of these children can explain or extend these patterns. In this task, students will identify, apply, and create alternating and more complex repeating patterns using geometric shapes. This serves as a way to incorporate a critical area of the geometry domain, which includes identifying and describing two-dimensional shapes (squares, triangles, and circles).

Strategies

- Students may chant the pattern out loud.
- Students may use a guess-and-check method, and then need to go back to the beginning of the pattern each time to determine if their pattern holds.

MISCONCEPTIONS/STUDENT DIFFICULTIES

- Students may not be able to extend the pattern, just repeating the last shape or randomly placing the mittens on the clothesline.
- Students may begin a pattern, but then forget it as they continue to extend the pattern.
- Students may not think about more complex repeating patterns, such as an ABB pattern.

LAUNCH

Begin the task by reading *Three Little Kittens* in the Mother Goose collection. Hand out the mitten manipulatives and ask students what shapes they see on the mittens. Questions to extend understanding beyond the patterning activity into the geometry domain could include the following:

- What do you know about triangles? How is a triangle different than a circle? How is a triangle different than a square? What do triangles and squares have in common?
- Can you find a triangle in this classroom?

Inform the students that all of the kittens at a local school went out to play on a snowy day. When the kittens returned to their classroom, they had to hang their mittens on the clothesline to dry. Post the following mitten pattern on a mock clothesline for the children to see. Ask students what they notice about the mittens on the line. Ask students which mitten will be next on the clothesline and how they know.

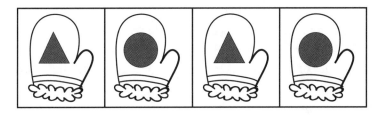

Ask students to describe this pattern using letters such as AB or ABB and so forth. Students may not have been asked to describe patterns in this way before. As needed, discuss how patterns are named using letters. Students of this age may struggle with this abstract representation of repeating patterns or with recognizing letters of the alphabet. Provide any necessary supports for this representation, and expect them to need several more experiences, beyond this problem, with naming patterns in this way.

Have students use the mittens to construct and extend the pattern if more kittens hang up their mittens. Ask students to come to the board to show the pattern for two additional iterations of the pattern core (a total of eight mittens). Ask students how many mittens are hanging on the clothesline now. Model counting to find the total number of mittens, or call on students to share their counting strategies, which may include using one-to-one correspondence, subitizing (including seeing eight as four and four), or counting by twos. Ask students which mitten they think will come next. Ask them to predict which mitten will be the tenth mitten; then have them verify their prediction by extending the pattern.

EXPLORE

Explain to students that they now get to hang up the kittens' mittens using any pattern and any number of mittens they would like. Read the task. Encourage students to create a different pattern from the one shown in class. Once students have completed their patterns, ask them to describe their pattern to a neighbor using descriptive words (e.g., *first, second, third*, etc.) and stating the type of pattern (e.g., AB, ABB, etc.) Some suggested sentence frames are listed below; students may fill in the blanks using pictures or words:

- My first mitten has a _____ on it.
- My second mitten has a _____ on it.
- My third mitten has a _____ on it.
- My pattern is an _____ pattern.

As children work, ask the following questions to check for understanding:

- How did you choose which mitten came next in your pattern?
- What do you notice about this pattern?
- What is the same about this pattern and the first pattern?
- What is different about this pattern and the first pattern?
- Why did you complete the pattern this way?
- What would be the next mitten? How do you know?
- What would the fifth to tenth mittens be? How do you know? (This number will depend upon students' abilities to count small quantities.)
- Are there more circles or triangles? Are there fewer circles or triangles? (Students may group mittens to facilitate counting.)
- Can you show me the part of your pattern that is repeating?
- How does your pattern help you know what shape will come next?
- How many of the mittens are circles? How many are triangles? How many are squares?

SUMMARIZE

Ask students to present their patterns of mittens to the entire class to see who created the same type of pattern. After each child shares his or her pattern, ask if there are other patterns that are similar. For example, if there is already an AB pattern on display, encourage children to find similarities with other AB patterns as they are described. Although an AB pattern of "circle, square" is different from an AB pattern of "triangle, square," the structure of the pattern is the same.

For each pattern structure (e.g., AB or ABC), ask students to translate the pattern in a new way. For example, "Can anyone tell me what an AB pattern would look like if we used different colors?" Sketch their ideas for these patterns in a visible location, and ask other students to discuss whether or not these ideas reflect the targeted pattern structure.

For some patterns (as time permits), ask the children what element would come next. Children can chant the pattern displayed together and continue the chant, thereby determining the next shape that would appear on the clothesline.

Throughout the discussion of patterns, you may want to include references to counting and comparison of the total numbers of mittens. Incorporating number sense concepts into this patterning activity can further reinforce counting and cardinality concepts:

Cardinality: How many mittens do you have on your clothesline? How many mittens with triangles do you have on your clothesline?

Comparison: Who has more mittens on the clothesline, you or your partner? How do you know?

If no student creates a more complex repeating pattern, such as an ABB pattern, pose the following task: Ask the students what the pattern would be if the kittens lined up their mittens by putting two circle mittens *after* each triangle mitten. Give a pattern strip to each child or team of two, and have students work with their partner to translate this statement into a pattern of "triangle, circle, circle, triangle, circle, circle" as shown below. After students have created their pattern, share it to ensure everyone made the correct pattern.

DIFFERENTIATION

- Chanting the pattern can assist struggling students with decomposing the pattern (Moomaw 2011).
- When students are creating their own patterns, limit or extend the types of mittens that the student can use to build a pattern.
- Begin a pattern with two mittens and have students decide how to continue the pattern.
- As an extension, students can use the blank mittens to create shapes other than the triangle, circle, and square. Similarly, they may use the same shape but different colors to create the pattern.
- After each pattern is shared, challenge students to determine which mitten would be in the twentieth position.

SLEDDING RACE

Snowflake Mountain had a sledding race. When sleds finished the race, they were given a number to show the order in which they crossed the finish line. Some were given numbers and some were given dots to show their place. When the last sled crossed the line, it crashed into all the other sleds. This caused a big pileup. Before the trophies can be given out, the sleds have to be placed in order. Can you help place the sleds in order from first place to last place?

CCSSM Standard for Mathematical Practice

Practice 7: Look for and make use of structure.

CCSSM Standards for Mathematical Content

K.CC.A.3: Write numbers from 0 to 20. Represent a number of objects with a written numeral 0–20 (with 0 representing a count of no objects).

K.CC.B.4: Understand the relationship between numbers and quantities; connect counting to cardinality.

Problem Discussion

Clements and Sarama (2009) identify four aspects of early numerical knowledge, which are highlighted in this problem:

1. Students must be able to recognize and name how many items are in a small set.
2. They should be able to use the names of numbers to order numbers in a sequence.
3. Children must be able to enumerate objects by verbalizing the number word that corresponds to each successive object.
4. Students should be able to determine that the total number of items is the same as the last number word verbalized (p. 23).

This activity provides students the opportunity to see that the numerical symbol for a number has a quantitative meaning, which is relevant to the context of this task (Clements and Sarama 2009). Students identify, read, and write numbers using a variety of representations in order to determine the quantity (Tobey and Fagan 2013). Through the use of dot patterns, young children can develop their ability to subitize, or quickly recognize how many are in a set without counting each object. Specifically, this task highlights two important types of subitizing: perceptual and conceptual (Clements 1999). *Perceptual subitizing* refers to the recognition of a "number without using other mathematical processes" (Ibid., p. 401). For example, a student sees the four-dot pattern on a die and automatically knows the quantity is four. *Conceptual subitizing* employs additional mathematical processes such as composing equal groups. For instance, a student looks at the four-dot patterns on two dice and sees eight as two groups of four. This problem also focuses on developing students' abilities to use efficient and systematic counting methods to determine the total count as well as to use rote counting to place numbers in order (K.CC.A.3).

As a precursor to the kindergarten counting and cardinality domain, students will explore the relationship between numbers and quantity by investigating how successive numbers in a sequence are related (SMP 7). For example, when counting by ones, each successive number represents a quantity that is one more than the previous number (K.CC.B.4).

STRATEGIES

- Students may either count the dots one by one or subitize to quickly find the total number of dots. For example, a student may see the sled with four dots and recognize four as two and two.
- Students may use counting strategies along with subitizing (e.g., count by twos). For instance, a student may see the sled with ten dots and mentally count "two, four, six, eight, ten."
- Students may use rote counting to determine the order of the sleds.
- Students may create dots for all the sleds and focus on the quantity of dots to place the sleds in order. For example, they may recognize three dots as more than two dots.

MISCONCEPTIONS/STUDENT DIFFICULTIES

- Students may miscount the number of dots (e.g., skipping or double counting dots).
- Students may write the number symbol incorrectly, such as writing the number backward.
- Students may not yet know the written number symbols for the quantities.
- Students may not understand that each successive number represents a quantity that is one larger than the previous number.

LAUNCH

To launch this task, ask students if they have ever been in a race and what kind of race it was. To ensure students have access to the academic language of order, such as *first, second, third,* and so forth, ask these questions to check for understanding:

- How do you know who wins the race?
- What does it mean if you got first place in a race? Second place?
- What does it mean to be in last place?

To demonstrate the idea of the order of the results of a race, students can be assigned a "place," and then asked to line up in order from first to fifth place.

Next, tell students their task today is related to a sled race. Ask how many of them have ridden on a sled. Ask if they have ever raced someone while sledding.

EXPLORE

Before reading the problem to the students, show them the sleds. Ask students what they notice about the sleds. Students should recognize that some sleds have a number on them and others have dots representing the sled's number. They should then be asked to complete each precut sled so that it has both a number and the corresponding number of dots.

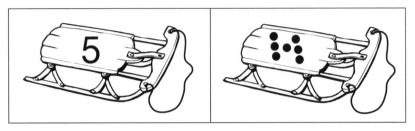

Ask the following questions to confirm understanding:

- How do you know you counted all the dots?
- How do you know that is the total number of dots? (The last number counted represents the total number of dots.)
- Is there another way to count the total number of dots (e.g., count by twos, subitize, and count on)?
- How did you know how many dots to make?

After students have completed their ten sleds, read the problem aloud. Next ask students to share a strategy for ordering the sleds from first place to tenth place with an elbow partner. Finally, students should use a shared strategy to complete this task individually or with their elbow partner.

Ask the following questions to check for understanding:

- Can you count from one to ten? How can you decide if a number is larger than another number?
- How do you know that three is a smaller number than four? How much smaller? Can you show me with the dots?

Attend to the different strategies students use to count and order their sleds. For example, do they apply one-to-one counting strategies or apply more sophisticated strategies such as subitizing or counting by twos or threes? During the Summarize phase, students could share their strategies in order of sophistication.

For students who are struggling to order the sleds, place two or more of the sleds in order for each student. For example, place sleds 3 and 8 in the correct spots, and then ask the student to place the others. Ask students questions like, "Can you show me which sled goes in first place?" "Do you know which number comes after four?" or "Do you know which number comes before three?"

SUMMARIZE

Have students share their strategies for finding the order of the sleds with a different partner. Ask students to present their strategies to the whole class. Ask questions to facilitate the discussion such as, "Did anyone else use this strategy?" "Did anyone use a different strategy?" Throughout the sharing of methods, attend to the different levels of counting techniques, from unorganized counting to a systematic counting strategy. For example, when asked how many are in the set, do students recognize that the last number verbalized represents the total quantity or do they count the entire set again? Do students recognize that when numbers are placed in order from smallest to largest, each successive number is one more than the previous number, or do they simply use the number "chant" to place numbers in order?

To ensure the sleds are in the correct order, ask a student to bring his or her first-place sled up to the front. Then ask another student to bring up the next sled. Ask how they know their sled is the next sled. Continue this process until all the sleds have been brought to the front.

Differentiation

- To support struggling students, use sleds 1 through 5.
- Provide struggling students with a single ten-frame or a double ten-frame so they can place sleds until all frames are filled.
- Some children may be able to order the sleds fairly quickly and easily. Challenge these students by asking "how many more or less" questions, such as "How many more is 8 than 5?" or "How many sleds will be between sled 5 and sled 8?"
- Another extension is to provide blank sleds and have students create the next few sleds.
- A modification for higher performing students may involve using some of the blank sleds in lieu of some of the numbered sleds. For example, replace sled 6 and sled 2 with blank sleds. The student would then have to determine which sleds are missing and create the two sleds.

Ms. Frost's Scarves

The students in Ms. Frost's room made special scarves for their class with numbers, pictures, and symbols on them. Some of the scarves have a sum of 10 and others do not. Some have missing numbers or pictures that have been worn away during recess.

There should be the same number of scarves that have a sum of 10 as there are scarves that do not have a sum of 10. Sort the scarves into two piles, those that make 10 and those that do not. You will have to complete some of the scarves that are missing numbers, pictures, and symbols.

CCSSM Standard for Mathematical Practice
Practice 2: Reason abstractly and quantitatively.

CCSSM Standards for Mathematical Content

K.OA.A.3 Decompose numbers less than or equal to 10 into pairs in more than one way, e.g., by using objects or drawings, and record each decomposition by a drawing or equation (e.g., 5 = 2 + 3 and 5 = 4 + 1).

K.OA.A.4 For any number from 1 to 9, find the number that makes 10 when added to the given number, e.g., by using objects or drawings, and record the answer with a drawing or equation.

K.NBT.A.1 Compose and decompose numbers from 11 to 19 into ten ones and some further ones, e.g., by using objects or drawings, and record each composition or decomposition by a drawing or equation (such as 18 = 10 + 8); understand that these numbers are composed of ten ones and one, two, three, four, five, six, seven, eight, or nine ones.

Problem Discussion

This problem focuses students' attention on the variety of ways to make ten. Students are challenged to decide which scarves show ten and which do not (K.OA.A.3 and K.OA.A.4). In some cases, students will need to find the missing addends to create their own scarves that equal ten and others that do not equal ten. Students will build on their understanding of counting and cardinality to solve these addition problems. This task provides opportunities for students to build on their abilities to compose and decompose numbers greater than ten (K.NBT.A.1). As students learn to solve these addition problems, they progress through levels of thinking from using direct modeling to counting strategies and, finally, to number facts (Dougherty et al. 2010). This task is designed to allow access to students at any of these levels. Through the use of different representations for the addends (dots and numbers), students are able to link subitizing skills to direct modeling and counting strategies.

This task also develops numerical fluency by focusing on students' progression of number concepts from concrete to abstract. Students working at the concrete level may count all by using counters to represent each numeral (or number of objects) and then counting all of the counters to find the sum. Other students may use a counting-on strategy by either counting on from the first addend (e.g., when solving 3 + 7, students start with three and count on seven more) or at a more sophisticated level, they may count on from the larger addend (e.g., when solving 3 + 7, students start with seven and count on three more). Some students may use part-whole reasoning to decompose one or more addends (e.g., when solving 3 + 7, students may decompose 7 into 2 and 5, and then add 3 more, knowing that 3 + 2 is 5 and 5 + 5 is 10). Finally, students may use relational thinking to find a sum (e.g., because 3 + 7 = 10, then 4 + 7 must be just one more than 10).

In this task, students must be able to solve a number sentence and recognize how their solution relates to the task at hand, which is to create number sentences that equal ten or do not equal ten. As such, young students begin to recognize that a specific quantity (e.g., five dots) can be represented using a numeral and vice versa (SMP 2). Another problem-solving aspect of this task is the condition that there be two groups of ten scarves. As such, students will need to fill in missing addends to create scarves that ensure an equal number in each pile. Blank scarves are included to allow for differentiation (see Differentiation section below).

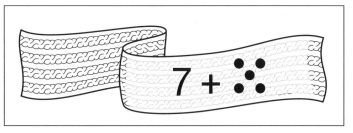

STRATEGIES

- Students may directly model the problem using concrete manipulatives or by drawing pictures to represent the sum and count all.
- Students may also use a counting-on strategy, especially when there is one numeral plus dots.
- Students may use a guess-and-check strategy.
- Students may use addition facts.
- Students may not need to calculate every sum in order to determine if it is equal to 10 or not. For example, a student may see 5 + 6, and instead of determining this is equal to 11, just note that 5 + 5 is 10, so 5 + 6 must not be equal to 10.
- Students may sort the completed scarves first, notice they need one more scarf that is not equal to 10, and create a scarf equal to 10 to ensure the piles are even. They will continue to alternate between the two piles until all the blank scarves are completed and distributed into one or the other pile.
- Students may compose or decompose numbers into known facts (e.g., make 5, make 10, doubles, doubles plus one, etc.). For example, students might solve 5 + 6 by decomposing or splitting apart 6 into 5 + 1 and use a doubles-plus-one strategy (5 + 5 = 10 and 10 + 1 = 11).

MISCONCEPTIONS/STUDENT DIFFICULTIES

- If students are using objects or drawing pictures, they may miscount the total number of objects.
- If students are using a counting-on or counting-down strategy, they may have a counting error such as counting on from six scarves by counting "six, seven, eight, nine, ten" and saying they need "five more scarves to make ten."

LAUNCH

Give each student a scarf like the one below with a missing addend. Tell them they will have to fill in the blank with a number, and also say, "You will need to decide if your scarf will sum to ten, or sum to more or less than ten." After students finish their scarf, share a variety of scarves and ask, "Is this scarf equal to ten, more than ten, or less than ten? How do you know?"

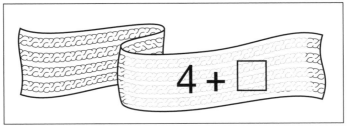

Next, partner up students and hand out the twenty scarves to each pair of students. Ask students to count how many total scarves they have. Then read the task to the students highlighting the fact that there are an equal number of scarves that sum to ten as there are scarves that do not sum to ten. Have students talk to their partner about what the task is asking them to do and what strategies they will use to complete the task. Ask partners to share their thoughts with the whole class. Prompt them to consider how many scarves will be in each pile (those that add to ten and those that do not). Restate their thoughts to make sure students understand there should be ten scarves in each pile.

EXPLORE

Have students work with their partner to complete the task.

Ask the following questions to check for understanding:

- How do you know that scarf makes (or does not make) ten?
- Does this scarf sum to more or less than ten? How do you know? Can you show me how you figured it out?
- How many scarves are in each of your piles? Do the piles have an equal number of scarves?

For students who are struggling to find the sum on the scarves, provide a single ten-frame and double ten-frame so students can use each square to place a manipulative or picture. Provide double ten-frames to encourage students to see that numbers eleven to nineteen can be decomposed into ten plus some more. Students struggling with the scarves with missing addends can be asked whether or not they want to create a sum of ten. Other scaffolding questions could include, "What would you have to add to (number) to have a sum of ten?" and "What would you have to add to (number) to have a sum less than (or more than ten)?" Attend to the different levels of sophistication of the counting strategies used from concrete to abstract (see Problem Discussion).

Summarize

Ask each student pair to find one scarf they created that does not sum to ten. Then make groups of four by joining pairs of students. Have each pair explain to the other how they know this scarf does not sum to ten. Then ask each pair to find a scarf that does sum to ten and have them explain to the other pair how they know the sum is ten. As students share their strategies with each other, attend to which counting strategies are used. Ask the pairs of students to tell each other how they made sure their two piles had the same number of scarves. Next, have the pairs swap all twenty scarves. They should sort the other pair's scarves, checking that each group (equal to ten and not equal to ten) has ten scarves.

To conclude the activity, select students to share their strategies with the whole class based on the level of sophistication. Ask questions to facilitate the discussion such as, "Did anyone else use this strategy?" "Did anyone use a different strategy?" Throughout the sharing of methods, ask students to compare the similarities and differences between strategies and which technique they would use the next time they had to solve a similar task.

Differentiation

- To support struggling students, allow the use of manipulatives and ten-frames.
- To support struggling students, only include sums that are less than ten.
- To extend this task, include scarves that have three addends, require subtraction, or are completely blank, allowing students to determine both addends.
- Another extension includes students sorting the scarves into different piles based on other characteristics, for example, three piles that are equal to ten, more than ten, and less than ten, or dots only, dots and numbers, and numbers only, and so on.

Snow Gear

After playing in the snow, Kylie and Kinley need to put away their snow gear.

(a) Use the picture of their garage to see if you can figure out where Kinley thinks they should place the scarves, hats, gloves, and boots. Here are some clues:

    Clue 1: The scarves are above the balls.

    Clue 2: The gloves are below the bike.

    Clue 3: The hats are next to the bike.

    Clue 4: The boots are between the rake and the garbage can.

(b) Now it is your turn to make clues for Kylie. Decide in which basket you think Kylie should place the scarves, hats, gloves, and boots. Use the sentences below to help you write your clues:

    The _____ are below the _____.

    The _____ are above the _____.

    The _____ are under the _____.

    The _____ are between the _____ and the _____.

CCSSM Standard for Mathematical Practice

Practice 6: Attend to precision.

CCSSM Standard for Mathematical Content

K.G.A.1: Describe objects in the environment using names of shapes, and describe the relative positions of these objects using terms such as *above, below, beside, in front of, behind,* and *next to.*

Problem Discussion

This task is designed to address spatial orientation by allowing students to choose where to place snow gear in a garage. Spatial orientation refers to how objects are related in space using positional language. Students will be asked to use spatial orientation to describe positions, such as *below, above, between,* and *next to.* Students first learn terms that describe location of objects, such as *in, on,* or *under,* and then to use words such as *next to, between,* and *beside* to describe spatial relationships (Clements and Sarama 2009; Moomaw 2011).

The first part of this task offers students two possible solution pathways. For example, the second clue states that the gloves are below the bike. Based on the other clues, there are two options for the basket in which the students can place the gloves. They can be placed directly below the bike or between the balls and garbage can. This allows for a class discussion about proximity. In part (b) of the task, students can practice this notion of objects being above or below another object but not necessarily *directly* above or below the item when they choose the location for storing each piece of gear. For example, placing the gloves in the basket that is directly below the bike could be described as "next to the bike," which would result in three potential locations for the gloves. The other clues would then have to help students narrow down these options.

One extension of this task requires students to describe the location of the snow gear in terms of shapes instead of the actual items in the garage. For example, students may rename objects such as balls and cans using the more formal language of *spheres* and *cylinders*, respectfully. Instead of saying, "The gloves are between the balls and the can," a student would say, "The gloves are between the spheres and the cylinder." According to the Progression for the Common Core State Standards for Mathematics, K–6 Geometry (Common Core Standards Writing Team 2012), kindergarten students are expected to be able to recognize several two-dimensional (squares, circles, triangles, rectangles) and three-dimensional (sphere, cube, cylinder, cone) shapes (K.G.1). This development of their understanding of the terminology for three-dimensional shapes, which appear in multiple forms, as well as for terms related to spatial orientation engages students in precise and accurate communication (SMP 6).

STRATEGIES

- Students may randomly place the objects and need to go back and check their work.
- Students may place the items directly above or below the indicated object.
- Students may realize objects do not need to be directly below or above the indicated object.

MISCONCEPTIONS/STUDENT DIFFICULTIES

- Students may have difficulty processing multiple clues to determine the correct location for each item or realizing that all clues must be true for the final arrangement of shapes.
- Students may struggle to understand the difference between words that imply direct contact and those that do not (e.g., *next to* implies direct contact, but *above* and *below* do not imply direct contact).

LAUNCH

Begin the task by showing students an arrangement of six items or shapes as in the example below. Tell students that they will be using this arrangement to describe the location of each object. Ask students to think of a way to describe the location of the triangle. Students may respond with a variety of statements such as the following:

- "The triangle is above the scarf." (Probe students to see if they recognize that the triangle is also above the circle and the pumpkin.)
- "The triangle is between the sled and the square (or the rectangle)."
- "The triangle is next to the sled (or the square or the rectangle)."

Ask students to share their descriptions and write the key terms, for instance, *next to*, *between*, *above*, *below*, and so forth, on the board for all to see. These terms will be used throughout the exploration of the task.

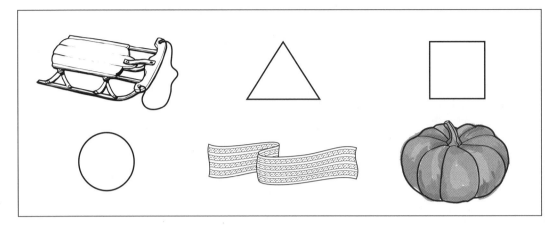

EXPLORE

Show students the picture of the garage. Ask students to talk to an elbow partner about the objects and shapes they see in the picture. Share some of their thoughts as a whole class. Tell students, "After playing in the snow, Kylie and Kinley need to put away their snow gear. They have scarves, hats, gloves, and boots to put away. There are five baskets in their garage. Each basket must hold the same items." Make sure students can identify the five baskets. Next, hand out one of each piece of snow gear to students. Ask students to hold up each piece of gear to make sure they know what each piece is called.

Read part (a) of the task. As you read the clues, have students place the gear in the appropriate basket. Then reread the clue for each item and have partners check each other's work to make sure the placement of the gear fits the clue. You may want to mention that there are different ways to satisfy some of the clues. For example, "The scarves are above the balls," could be solved by placing the scarves in either of the baskets that are beside the bike. Also mention that once an item is placed, they may need to change that location on the basis of future clues.

After the class has completed part (a) of the task, ask individual students to present their answers. Reread each clue and as a class decide if the student's solution satisfies each clue. Do this for the different solutions students find.

SUMMARIZE

Have students complete part (b) of the task individually. Remind them that each basket must hold the same items. Students then trade clues with their partners and place the items based on the partner's clues. To conclude, share clues from a few students and allow the whole class to solve the task. Next, ask partners to talk to each other about their strategies for creating the clues and placing the snow gear. Have students share their thoughts with the whole class.

DIFFERENTIATION

- To support struggling students, help them place one or two items, and focus only on the last clues.

- To support struggling students, have them create only two clues for part (b).

- To extend this task, ask students to create their own picture of a garage with baskets. Have them create clues about the garage for another student to solve.

- To extend this task, have students describe the location of the snow gear in terms of shapes instead of the actual items in the garage. For example, students use the formal words *sphere* and *cylinder* rather than ball and cans, respectively.

Sledding Fun

The first-grade class went to Snowflake Mountain on a field trip. Twenty of the students wanted to go sledding. There were 3 types of sleds. There were 5-person sleds, 3-person sleds, and 1-person sleds. Using pictures and equations, how many ways can you find so that all 20 students can go sledding with no empty seats?

CCSSM Standard for Mathematical Practice

Practice 4: Model with mathematics.

CCSSM Standards for Mathematical Content

1.OA.A.2: Solve word problems that call for addition of three whole numbers whose sum is less than or equal to 20, e.g., by using objects, drawings, and equations with a symbol for the unknown number to represent the problem.

1.OA.B.3: Apply properties of operations as strategies to add and subtract. Examples: If 8 + 3 = 11 is known, then 3 + 8 = 11 is also known (commutative property of addition). To add 2 + 6 + 4, the second two numbers can be added to make a ten, so 2 + 6 + 4 = 2 + 10 = 12 (associative property of addition).

Problem Discussion

This task gives students the occasion to solve an addition problem with three or more addends using a variety of strategies (1.OA.A.2). The featured strategies allow learners at different levels of understanding to have access to the task through the use of concrete manipulatives, pictorial representations, or abstract equations. In the early grades, students should be offered opportunities to model real-world addition and subtraction situations using these techniques (SMP 4). For example, prior to first grade, students have developed an understanding that numbers can be decomposed in a variety of ways, such as 5 = 2 + 3, 5 = 1 + 4, and 5 = 5 + 0.

Students in first grade are encouraged to use an assortment of addition strategies. These vary in sophistication from concrete to abstract. In this situation, concrete strategies may include the use of counters to represent the number of students on each sled; then counting all to ensure all 20 students are on a sled; for example, a child may set out 3 groups of 5 counters, 1 group of 3 counters, and 2 separate counters for 2 one-person sleds to represent the 20 first graders on sleds. Other students may use a counting-on strategy by starting to count by fives to quickly see that 3 five-person sleds represent 15 students, and then count on from 15 to find the remaining number of first graders who still need a sled. Or students may use strategies related to decomposition of numbers to help them find the needed number of sleds. For example, after selecting 3 five-person sleds, they may decompose the remaining 5 students into 3 and 2, and realize they can use 1 three-person sled and 2 one-person sleds. Students may also apply both the commutative and associative properties of addition (1.OA.B.3) by recognizing that the order in which they count the number of students on each sled does not matter.

Students must use quantitative reasoning to attend to the meaning of the different quantities involved in this task—the number of each type of sled and the number of students that each kind of sled will hold. By creating an organized list, students can build on their problem-solving skills and determine if they have exhausted all solutions. The table below represents the total number of different ways that the first-grade class could rent sleds for their field trip.

Number of 5-Person Sleds	Number of 3-Person Sleds	Number of 1-Person Sleds	Equation
4	0	0	$5 + 5 + 5 + 5 = 20$
3	1	2	$5 + 5 + 5 + 3 + 1 + 1 = 20$
3	0	5	$5 + 5 + 5 + 1 + 1 + 1 + 1 + 1 = 20$
2	3	1	$5 + 5 + 3 + 3 + 3 + 1 = 20$
2	2	4	$5 + 5 + 3 + 3 + 1 + 1 + 1 + 1 = 20$
2	1	7	$5 + 5 + 3 + 1 + 1 + 1 + 1 + 1 + 1 + 1 = 20$
2	0	10	$5 + 5 + 10 = 20$
1	5	0	$5 + 3 + 3 + 3 + 3 + 3 = 20$
1	4	3	$5 + 3 + 3 + 3 + 3 + 1 + 1 + 1 = 20$
1	3	6	$5 + 3 + 3 + 3 + 1 + 1 + 1 + 1 + 1 + 1 = 20$
1	2	9	
1	1	12	
1	0	15	
0	6	2	
0	5	5	
0	4	8	
0	3	11	
0	2	14	
0	1	17	
0	0	20	

STRATEGIES

- Students may use a guess-and-check strategy.
- Students may use manipulatives to help them find the answer.
- Students may use counting strategies such as counting all, counting on, or skip counting.
- Students may break the problem down and make combinations to 10 and simply repeat these combinations.
- Students may use missing addends strategies, for instance, grouping the 20 students on two 5-person sleds and two 3-person sleds, and then solving 16 + _____ = 20.

MISCONCEPTIONS/STUDENT DIFFICULTIES

- Students may write equations to model the total number of sleds rather than the total number of people.
- Students may not be able to transition from the concrete or representational phase to the abstract phase of writing the equations.
- Students may not recognize the commutative property and double-count situations, for example, counting 5 + 5 + 3 + 3 + 3 + 1 and 3 + 3 + 3 + 5 + 5 + 1 as two different sets of sleds.

LAUNCH

Begin the task by asking students how many of them have ridden on a sled. Discuss how some sleds are made to carry one person while others can carry more than one person. Ask if anyone has ever been on a sled that carried more than one person. If so, ask how many people could fit on the sled. Bring seven children to the front of the room. Ask students to think of a way these seven classmates could sled down a hill. Encourage students to go beyond one-person sleds or a limit of two sleds. Some examples include a four-person sled and a three-person sled or 2 three-person sleds and a one-person sled. Use the children to model a few of the situations, and ask students to write equations to represent each situation. Students may question whether changing the order of the children in the sled would result in a "different" sled. For this task, we suggest counting the sled just one time. To demonstrate the commutative property, have the children representing the three-person sled switch position with their classmates modeling the four-person sled; then rewrite the equation to discuss whether 3 + 4 is the same as 4 + 3 in this context.

EXPLORE

Read the task to the students. Students can work individually or in pairs to solve the task. As students record their pictures and equations, encourage them to find all possible ways the twenty students could sled down the hill.

Ask these questions to check for understanding:

- How do you know all the students were able to ride on a sled?
- How many sleds of each kind did you use? Is there another way the students could sled down the hill?
- Could you explain to me how your equation represents the number of students and the number of sleds?
- What if you used 2 five-person sleds? How many more students need to get on sleds? Which type of sleds can you use for those students?

SUMMARIZE

Ask students to discuss their strategies for solving the task with their partner or another student pair. As students share their strategies with the entire class, ask questions like, "How many of you used a similar strategy?" "How was your strategy similar to or different from this one?" Encourage them to consider which strategies would be efficient in helping find all possible solutions. One strategy may be to find all combinations using five-person sleds as explored in the table above. Another is to find combinations that use only one type of sled, two types of sleds, and, finally, all types of sleds as shown in the equations below.

Next, ask students to share and record their equations for everyone to see, beginning with those students who used only one type of sled and proceeding to students who used two types and then to those who used three types of sleds. Below is a complete list of possible equations. Throughout the discussion, attend to the difference between the total number of sleds and the total number of students on the sleds. Also focus students' attention on strategies for adding more than two numbers by first adding numbers that group to ten or five. For example, if a student writes 5 + 1 + 3 + 3 + 3 + 5 = 20, rewrite the problem as 5 + 5 + 3 + 3 + 3 + 1 = 20 and then verify this is the same as 20 by adding the 2 fives and then skip-counting by threes to get nine and then adding one more to get 20 (i.e., 5 + 5 = 10; skip-counting 3, 6, 9, + 1 = 10; 10 + 10 = 20.)

As students share their equations, ask the class to rewrite the equations so that numbers are in an order that allows them to easily make groups of five or ten. Ask them to determine the arrangement of students that uses the most number of sleds and the fewest number of sleds.

Equations using one type of sled are as follows:

1 + 1 + 1 + 1 + 1 + 1 + 1 + 1 + 1 + 1 + 1 + 1 + 1 + 1 + 1 + 1 + 1 + 1 + 1 + 1 = 20
5 + 5 + 5 + 5 = 20

Equations using two types of sleds are as follows:

1 + 1 + 1 + 1 + 1 + 1 + 1 + 1 + 1 + 1 + 1 + 1 + 1 + 1 + 1 + 1 + 1 + 3 = 20
1 + 1 + 1 + 1 + 1 + 1 + 1 + 1 + 1 + 1 + 1 + 1 + 1 + 1 + 3 + 3 = 20
1 + 1 + 1 + 1 + 1 + 1 + 1 + 1 + 1 + 1 + 1 + 3 + 3 + 3 = 20
1 + 1 + 1 + 1 + 1 + 1 + 1 + 1 + 3 + 3 + 3 + 3 = 20
1 + 1 + 1 + 1 + 1 + 3 + 3 + 3 + 3 + 3 = 20
1 + 1 + 3 + 3 + 3 + 3 + 3 + 3 = 20
1 + 1 + 1 + 1 + 1 + 1 + 1 + 1 + 1 + 1 + 1 + 1 + 1 + 1 + 1 + 5 = 20
1 + 1 + 1 + 1 + 1 + 1 + 1 + 1 + 1 + 1 + 5 + 5 = 20
1 + 1 + 1 + 1 + 1 + 5 + 5 + 5 = 20
3 + 3 + 3 + 3 + 3 + 5 = 20

Equations using all three types of sleds are as follows:

$1 + 1 + 1 + 1 + 1 + 1 + 1 + 1 + 1 + 1 + 1 + 3 + 5 = 20$

$1 + 1 + 1 + 1 + 1 + 1 + 1 + 1 + 1 + 3 + 3 + 5 = 20$

$1 + 1 + 1 + 1 + 1 + 1 + 3 + 3 + 3 + 5 = 20$

$1 + 1 + 1 + 3 + 3 + 3 + 3 + 5 = 20$

$1 + 1 + 1 + 1 + 1 + 1 + 1 + 3 + 5 + 5 = 20$

$1 + 1 + 1 + 1 + 3 + 3 + 5 + 5 = 20$

$1 + 3 + 3 + 3 + 5 + 5 = 20$

$1 + 1 + 3 + 5 + 5 + 5 = 20$

Differentiation

- To support students who struggle, provide them with manipulatives or representations such as double ten-frames, rekenreks, counters, or a number line to add the multiple addends.
- To support students who struggle, decrease the number of students on sleds to ten or fifteen.
- To modify the task, provide an equation leaving out one or more of the addends. Have students use manipulatives to find the missing addends.
- To extend the task, ask students to determine all possible sled combinations.
- To extend the task, have students use ten sleds. Ask them if there is more than one way to use ten sleds.
- Ask students if it is possible to have an odd number of sleds being used.

Inches of Snowfall

Our friends in La Crosse, Wisconsin, have given us clues to determine the total number of inches of snowfall for the winter months of December, January, February, and March. Use these clues to determine snowfall amounts for each month. Make a bar graph to display your data.

Clue 1: The snowfall in December was 16 inches.

Clue 2: No month had the same amount of snowfall as any other month.

Clue 3: The total number of inches of snowfall for January and February was the same as the number of inches of snowfall in December.

Clue 4: It snowed 4 fewer inches in March than in February.

CCSSM Standards for Mathematical Practice

Practice 3: Construct viable arguments and critique the reasoning of others.

Practice 5: Use appropriate tools strategically.

CCSSM Standards for Mathematical Content

1.OA.A.1: Use addition and subtraction within 20 to solve word problems involving situations of adding to, taking from, putting together, taking apart, and comparing, with unknowns in all positions, e.g., by using objects, drawings, and equations with a symbol for the unknown number to represent the problem.

1.MD.C.4: Organize, represent, and interpret data with up to three categories; ask and answer questions about the total number of data points, how many in each category, and how many more or less are in one category than in another.

Problem Discussion

In this task students are given clues to an operations and algebraic-thinking word problem to create a bar graph. These clues, as well as the discussion questions, initiate adding to, taking from, putting together, taking apart, and comparing with unknowns in different positions for numbers within twenty (1.OA.A.1). The task also incorporates content related to data; students create a bar graph with four categories to display measurement data related to inches of snowfall (1.MD.C.4). In kindergarten, students are expected to classify, sort, and count data in categories (K.MD.B.3). These students display data using tally marks to represent counts of a particular category as well as employ physical objects to make graphs. This extends to first and second grades, when students create picture graphs and bar graphs. By the end of second grade students should be able to organize, represent, and interpret data by using counts and tallies and to create picture graphs and bar graphs (2.MD.D.10). This task provides a bridge between these kindergarten and second-grade standards by having students determine the counts for each category on the basis of the clues and operations and algebraic thinking. Students may also choose to use manipulatives and square-inch grid paper to create a graphical display summarizing the data (SMP 5). Manipulatives allow students to use trial-and-error strategies to determine if the clues are satisfied or if they need to reassess their thinking. The manipulatives can also be used to assist in the creation of the bar graphs.

This open-ended task offers students the opportunity to organize data and make comparisons among categories. A variety of answers is possible because the sixteen total inches for January and February can be shared in a number of ways as long as clues 2 and 4 are satisfied. For example, January and February cannot both have eight inches of snow, and February must have at least four inches of snow. During the summary, students are asked to share their graphs and justify how their quantities satisfy the given clues as well as respond to the arguments of others (SMP 3). In the event students choose four inches for February and twelve inches for January, there will be zero inches for March. This situation allows the discussion to focus on contexts where zero is a reasonable answer.

STRATEGIES

- Students may use manipulatives (e.g., linking cubes, counters, etc.) or 11 x 17 square-inch grid paper to directly model each clue in order to determine the height of the bars for each month.

- To find the number of inches of snowfall in January and February, the students may decompose 16 into doubles and then use a "one-up, one-down" strategy to satisfy clues 2 and 3.

- To find the number of inches of snowfall in January and February, the students may decompose 16 into 10 and 6.

- Student may guess a number of inches for January, and then use a missing-addends approach or take-from approach to find the total number of inches for February. For example, if students guess 6 inches of snow for January, a missing-addends strategy would include students thinking, "What do I have to add to 6 to get to 16?" Whereas a take-away plan would include students thinking, "What number is 16 take away 6?"

- Students may use a take-from approach to find the total number of inches of snowfall for March.

- Students may use a guess-and-check strategy to find the number of inches of snowfall for March.

- Student may begin with clue 4, choose the number of inches of snowfall in March, and work backward to find the amount of snowfall in January and February.

MISCONCEPTIONS/STUDENT DIFFICULTIES

- Students may not be able to think beyond an equal-groups plan to the both-addends-unknown clue (clue 3).

- Students may have difficulty with the terms *fewer* and *more than*.

- Students may have a difficult time creating graphs without the use of manipulatives or square-inch grid paper to show the one-to-one correspondence of the number of inches to the units on the graph.

- Students may count the lines on the square-inch grid paper instead of the spaces between the lines.

Launch

Begin with the statement, "The Weather Channel reported that the first snowfall of December in La Crosse, Wisconsin, was twelve inches of snow." Students may have heard phrases like "three inches of snow" on the news or in discussions at home. To help students understand the context involved in this task ask students, "Can you show me with your hands how deep you think the snow is in La Crosse?" Provide students with inch units and ask them to use the units to show how high twelve inches of snow is. Say, "Our friends in La Crosse said that by the end of December there was a total snowfall of sixteen inches. How much more snow fell since the first snowfall?" Encourage students to use manipulatives or pictorial representations to share their reasoning.

Explore

Explain to students that they are going to be working with a partner to graph the total amount of snow that fell during the winter months in La Crosse. Ask questions such as, "What are important parts of a graph?" "What could be the title of the graph?" Draw the vertical and horizontal axes of a graph and ask, "If we were graphing the snowfall in La Crosse, what label would go here (point to the horizontal axis, then the vertical axis)? How could we graph the amount of snowfall for December?"

Read the task to the class. Provide pairs of students with a sheet of 11 x 17 square-inch grid paper to begin the creation of a bar graph to represent the total amount of snowfall. As students work with their partner to create their graph, ask the following questions to assess for understanding:

- Can you show me on your graph the sixteen inches of snow that fell in December?
- How did you use these sixteen inches of snow for December to help you determine how many inches fell in January and February?
- Is it possible that the same amount of snow fell in January and February?
- Which month had the most snowfall?
- Which month had more snowfall, March or February? How much more?
- What is the fewest number of inches that could fall in February?
- Is it possible to have four inches fall in February?

Remind students to include important parts of the graph that were discussed in this part of the lesson (title and labels on the axes).

Summarize

To start the discussion, say, "I'm wondering if all of you have the same graph. Before we share, what do you think? Do you think everyone is going to have the same information on their graphs?" Have the pairs of students form groups of four to share their graphs. Ask each pair to explain how each piece of their graph satisfies each clue. The clues could be read to the whole class one by one if needed. To further discuss the variety of graphs and how students chose the quantities for their graph, ask the following questions:

- From the clues, what things had to be true?
- How did you make sure your quantities worked?
- What are the minimum values that might work?
- What are the maximum values that might work?
- Other than December, is it possible that January, February, or March could have more than sixteen inches of snow?

Select a graph to share with the whole class. Ask the following questions about the chosen graph to check for understanding:

- Which month had the least snowfall?
- How many more inches of snow fell in _____ than in _____?
- How many fewer inches of snow fell in _____ than in _____?
- How many total inches of snow fell in all four months? (This encourages students to share a variety of strategies, such as using the manipulatives to count all, making groups of ten, and skip counting.)
- What is another clue we could add that fits this graph? (Encourage a variety of clues, such as "_____inches of snow fell in February. _____ more inches of snow fell in December than in _____.")

DIFFERENTIATION

- To support students who struggle, the total amount of snowfall in December can be decreased.
- To support students who struggle, provide them with manipulatives to make their graphs by tracing them onto an 11 x 17 square-inch sheet of grid paper.
- To support struggling students, remove clue 2.
- To challenge students, add a clue 5: "Six more inches of snow fell in January than in February" or "There was one month in which no snow fell."
- Extend this task by asking students to create an additional clue for the amount of snowfall that matches their graph.

Super Bowl Sunday!

In Super Bowl XLVIII (48), the Denver Broncos faced the Seattle Seahawks for a football show-down. During the game, the quarterback for the Seattle Seahawks made 3 runs with the ball. Three runs (Run 1, Run 2, and Run 3) are marked with blue tape in the hallway. Can you put the runs in order from shortest to longest? Explain how you know your comparison is correct.

CCSSM Standards for Mathematical Practice

Practice 1: Make sense of problems and persevere in solving them.

Practice 5: Use appropriate tools strategically.

CCSSM Standards for Mathematical Content

1.MD.A.1: Order three objects by length; compare the lengths of two objects indirectly by using a third object.

1.MD.A.2: Express the length of an object as a whole number of length units, by laying multiple copies of a shorter object (the length unit) end to end; understand that the length measurement of an object is the number of same-size length units that span it with no gaps or overlaps. *Limit to contexts where the object being measured is spanned by a whole number of length units with no gaps or overlaps.*

Problem Discussion

Before engaging first graders in this problem, students ought to be able to compare objects by length using direct comparison and employ appropriate language (e.g., *longer, shorter*) to make comparative statements (K.MD.A.2). This problem requires students to move beyond this standard to the comparison of three objects that cannot be directly compared.

In this problem, students are required to seriate the three lengths (runs) from shortest to longest, but they are unable to place the three objects next to each other (1.MD.A.1). Thus, students will need to identify another means of comparison. Students will not be able to directly compare the lengths that have been marked, but they may use materials that allow them to make these comparisons (SMP 5). For example, they may cut a string the same length as Run 1, and then compare this string to Run 2 and Run 3 to determine the comparative relationship. Although this may help to identify the relationship between some runs, the students may struggle to find the comparative relationship between Run 2 and Run 3. If this situation is problematic for them, the students should be encouraged to seek alternative possibilities or to consider how they might expand on their current use of the tool to clear this hurdle.

Alternatively, students may choose to iterate a unit to identify a *measure* of each of the run lengths (1.MD.A.2). There is a wide range of possibilities for the unit: a student's stride length or body length, the length of a shoe, a 12-inch ruler, a length of string, a meter or yardstick, a book, linking cubes, paper clips, square tiles, and so on. Again, students should be encouraged to consider multiple possibilities. If an inefficient choice is made initially (e.g., square tiles), they may reconsider their choice of tool (SMP 1, SMP 5).

Note that it is not the intention of this problem to *require* students to use a nonstandard unit to measure the lengths of the runs. Instead, students should be encouraged to brainstorm possibilities for making the comparison and follow through on at least one of these. This problem may ultimately set up the *need* for length measurement, but students should see multiple options for tools that facilitate this comparison.

Historical Note: During Super Bowl XLVIII, Russell Wilson did indeed make three runs, totaling twenty-six yards. The length of each run in this problem, however, is not accurate to that statistic. The lengths have been manipulated to provide a more challenging comparison situation.

Problem Setup

Prior to the lesson, mark three different lengths on the floor in a school hallway. Using blue painter's tape, make the following three runs:

Run 1 = 10 yards
Run 2 = 7 yards
Run 3 = 9 yards

Provide some distance between the runs, so they are not easily compared. The runs may be set up in different hallways, but if this is not possible, consider the setup below in the same hallway. Setting up two or more sets of the runs may alleviate congestion.

Run 1	Run 2	Run 3
————	————	————

Strategies

- Students may use a single long object (e.g., cashier's tape, string) against which they can mark the different lengths and determine the order.
- Students may cut an object (e.g., cashier's tape, string) to the length of one run and compare this length against the other runs.
- Nonstandard units of measure (e.g., strides, body lengths, paper clips, linking cubes) may be laid end to end to determine the length of each run. Then students will determine the comparison based on the number of units for each run.
- Standard units of measure (e.g., 12-inch rulers, yardsticks) may be laid end to end to determine the length of each of the runs. Then students will determine the comparison based on the number of standard units for each run.

- One or two nonstandard linear units of measure (e.g., strides, body lengths, paper clips, linking cubes) may be iterated to determine the length of each run. Then students will determine the comparison based on the number of units for each run.
- One or two standard units of measure (e.g., 12-inch rulers, yardsticks) may be iterated to determine the length of each run. Then students will determine the comparison based on the number of standard units for each run.

Misconceptions/Student Difficulties

- Students may struggle with comparison terminology. For example, instead of saying *longer* or *shorter*, students may use *bigger* and *smaller*.
- After a string or cashier's tape is cut to equal the length of a run, students may only know the other runs in comparison to that length but not in comparison to each other.
- Students may choose a nonstandard unit of measure that is inefficient; for example, using Unifix cubes to measure a length of seven yards is challenging!
- Students may choose to use different units for each of the runs, making the measures incomparable. For example, they may use one student's foot for Run 1 and another student's foot for Run 2. Unless the feet are equal in length, these measures cannot be compared accurately.
- Nonstandard or standard units may be iterated along the length of each run, but students may fail to start at one end or to iterate the unit without gaps or overlaps. This will lead to an inaccurate measurement.

Launch

Ask students how many of them plan to watch the Super Bowl, and if they know what teams are participating in the upcoming game. Students may not have a wide range of knowledge about American football, so it would be helpful to discuss how the game is played.

Next, remind students that they have previously learned about comparing the lengths of objects. Choose two objects (e.g., pencils) to hold up for the class. Ask a student to demonstrate how we might compare the lengths of the two objects. When the student aligns the objects, ask other students to say a comparative sentence, for example, "The red pencil is shorter than the blue pencil," or "The blue pencil is longer than the red pencil." Ask, "How did putting the objects next to each other help us make that comparison?"

After students have revisited the idea of direct comparison, explain that today the students will be asked to compare the lengths of three objects that they cannot put next to each other. Read the problem context aloud to the students: "In Super Bowl XLVIII (48), the Denver Broncos faced the Seattle Seahawks for a football showdown. During the game, the quarterback for the Seattle Seahawks made three runs with the ball." Then ask students, "What is a run?" and "Why would a quarterback run with the ball instead of passing it?" Discuss the problem situation to ensure that the context itself is not an obstacle for the students.

Read the task aloud to students, and bring the class into the hallway to see the runs that have been marked in blue tape. It may be fruitful to ask students to make a prediction about which run is the longest and which is the shortest.

Back in the classroom, explain to students that they will work in groups of two to four to solve this problem. Before returning to the hall, ask students to brainstorm ideas for how they might compare the lengths of the runs, and encourage them to consider what tools and other materials available in the room they might use.

EXPLORE

Students should spend several minutes as a group identifying a plan for how they will compare the lengths of the three runs. Ask students to clear their plan with you or an assistant prior to going out into the hall. This is not to encourage a particular strategy, such as producing a measure, but to confirm that students have a tangible plan, have thought through their plan, and have the necessary materials.

Encourage students to create a recording sheet that corresponds with their plan. Also recommend that this recording sheet have an area where the group, whether using nonstandard or standard units, can record an estimate of how many units long each run is.

As students brainstorm how to make the comparison, refrain from making suggestions, offering insights, or giving criticisms. As needed, ask questions like the following to help students clarify their plan:

- How are you planning to use the (materials)?
- Can you explain how this method will help you determine which run is the longest?
- How will you know which run is the middle length?
- How are you planning to keep count? Who will record your data?
- How many of these (materials) do you think you might need?

If a group seems prepared to proceed with their plan, send them to the hallway to implement it. Tell all the groups that if they find they would like to revise their plans as they work, they may do so.

While students are working in the hallway, take note of the strategies they use to make appropriate comparisons. If possible, take pictures of students working and take note of the groups' solution strategies. When groups have finished their comparisons, ask them to prepare themselves for a presentation of their strategy. Additional options for extensions are provided in the Differentiation section.

Summarize

In a whole-group discussion, first ask who was able to determine how to order the runs from shortest to longest. Ask one student to share her results, and write them on the board. If there are alternative solutions, list these outcomes on the board as well.

Then ask a group to justify its ordering of the runs and fully explain how they made the comparisons between the lengths. Students in the audience may turn and talk to neighbors to process the strategy and ask questions of the group for further clarification.

Ask groups who solved the problem in a similar way to share their strategies. Highlight connections between groups that used a single long object to mark lengths. Similarly, highlight connections between groups that made a length equivalent to one of the runs, and then used this length as comparison to the other two runs.

For groups that used a unit to generate measures of the three lengths, record their measurements for the three runs in a table, with appropriate unit labels. Ask the class the following questions as appropriate:

- How did they use the units to find their measurements? (Did they iterate a unit or lay units end to end until the distance was covered?)
- What was important about the way they placed their units? (Did they attend to the end-to-end placement without gaps or overlaps?)
- Why did Group A and Group B get different measurements for the runs?
- Group C used a longer object to measure the runs. Why does this group have smaller measurements?
- Groups D and E used the same object to measure the runs. Should they have gotten the same measurements? Why do you think there are differences in their data?
- How did these measurements help you determine how to order the runs from shortest to longest?

If it is possible to share pictures taken of the group work in the Explore section, use these to illustrate and support each group's explanation. In addition, use photos of groups that specifically generated measures of the three runs to demonstrate this process to other groups that did not. If appropriate at this time, highlight procedures that are important to obtaining accurate measures, such as starting at one end and iterating the unit with no gaps or overlaps.

Differentiation

- For groups that are struggling to identify a way to make a comparison, ask them how cashier's tape or string might be used as a tool.
- Students could be asked to compare two of the lengths, Runs 1 and 2, Runs 2 and 3, or Runs 1 and 3. The class as a whole could then use this information to seriate all three runs from shortest to longest.

- For groups that finish quickly, prepare one or two additional runs in another hallway. Have these groups include these lengths with the other three to be ordered from shortest to longest.
- Challenge students to predict what would happen to the measurements if they used a different size unit. Have them carry out the measurements and explain the impact of using smaller or larger measurement units.

A POCKET FULL OF COINS

Caleb had some coins in his pocket. He noticed that the coins he had showed images of four different presidents: Lincoln, Jefferson, Roosevelt, and Washington. He counted the coins and found that he had a total of $1.25. Using the following clues, determine how many of each coin Caleb could have in his pocket:

Clue 1: Caleb has fewer coins with President Jefferson than President Roosevelt.

Clue 2: He has an odd number of coins with President Washington on them.

Clue 3: He has fewer than 40 coins with President Lincoln on them.

CCSSM STANDARDS FOR MATHEMATICAL PRACTICE

Practice 1: Make sense of problems and persevere in solving them.

Practice 2: Reason abstractly and quantitatively.

CCSSM STANDARDS FOR MATHEMATICAL CONTENT

2.MD.C.8: Solve word problems involving dollar bills, quarters, dimes, nickels, and pennies using $ and ¢ symbols appropriately. *Example: If you have 2 dimes and 3 pennies, how many cents do you have?*

2.NBT.B.6: Add up to four two-digit numbers using strategies based on place value and properties of operations.

PROBLEM DISCUSSION

This problem focuses on the concepts of currency and the images of the presidents on each coin. According to Clements and Sarama (2009), the development of skills related to money takes time because a variety of counting strategies are involved, including counting on and skip counting by fives, tens, and twenty-fives. In addition, students must recall the value of each coin and the name associated with it as well as be able to translate between dollars and cents. In this task, students apply this knowledge to find different combinations of coins that sum to $1.25 on the basis of clues that involve concepts of *less than* and *even and odd numbers*. As such, students need to translate between the currency symbols to recognize that 125¢ is the same as $1.25 (2.MD.C.8). Students also need to recognize that they can use different combinations of coins to result in the same amount of money. In addition, students apply different strategies for multidigit addition to solve this task (2.NBT.B.6). These include making combinations of ten and adding values in descending order.

To access this task, students must analyze the given constraints to develop possible solution strategies. They may look for entry points by using actual coins to make sense of the problem-solving task (SMP 1). In addition, students need to translate between two quantities: the number of each coin and the value of each coin. Transitioning between numbers and values enables students to contextualize the situation (SMP 2). Through whole-class discussion, students explore the structure of the currency system. Van de Walle, Karp, and Bay-Williams suggest coin-related lessons "should focus on purchase power— a dime can *buy the same thing* that 10 pennies can buy" (2010, p. 385). Questions of this nature during the launch of this activity can help students recognize patterns such as one less nickel results in five more pennies. This structure can be illustrated in a table similar to the one below, showing all coin combinations that are possible solutions for this task. Students will have the opportunity to discuss *purchase power* as they explore how they could exchange one type of coin for other types of coins, for example, exchanging one dime for one nickel and five pennies (shown in the transition from Row 1 to Row 2). It is important for students to understand that the task constraints limit the exchange of some quantities and possible coin combinations. This will make it necessary for students to check the reasonableness of their results using a variety of counting or addition strategies (SMP 1).

	Q	D	N	P	Total
Row 1	3	4	1	5	$1.25
Row 2	3	3	2	10	$1.25
Row 3	3	3	1	15	$1.25
Row 4	3	2	1	25	$1.25
Row 5	1	9	1	5	$1.25
Row 6	1	8	2	10	$1.25
Row 7	1	8	1	15	$1.25
Row 8	1	7	3	15	$1.25
Row 9	1	7	2	20	$1.25
Row 10	1	7	1	25	$1.25
Row 11	1	6	5	15	$1.25
Row 12	1	6	4	20	$1.25
Row 13	1	6	3	25	$1.25
Row 14	1	6	2	30	$1.25
Row 15	1	6	1	35	$1.25
Row 16	1	5	4	30	$1.25
Row 17	1	5	3	35	$1.25

STRATEGIES

- Students may randomly guess and check until they have a sum of $1.25, and then verify if the number of each coin meets the criteria.
- Students may begin by using the information about the quarters and realize there can only be one or three quarters.
- Once students find one solution, they recognize that in some situations they can break apart one value to find another solution. For example, they can trade in a dime for ten pennies while keeping the number of quarters and nickels the same.

- Students may apply counting strategies such as counting on and skip counting to quickly find the sum.

- Students may add values in random order (e.g., 1 + 10 + 5 + 1 + 1 + 25 + 1 + 1) rather than adding them in ascending or descending order (e.g., 25 + 10 + 5 +1 + 1 + 1 + 1 + 1).

- Students may write the total value of each type of coin in cents and then add the four addends together; for example, 3 quarters, 3 dimes, 2 nickels, and 10 pennies is translated as 75 + 30 + 10 + 10.

- Students may write each value for each type of coin and add the multiple addends together; for example, 3 quarters, 3 dimes, 2 nickels, and 10 pennies is translated as 25 + 25 + 25 + 10 + 10 + 10 + 5 + 5 + 1 + 1 + 1 + 1 + 1 + 1 + 1 + 1 + 1 + 1.

Misconceptions/Student Difficulties

- Students may not know the value or the name of each coin.

- Students may not verify or may have difficulty verifying that their sum is made up of numbers of coins that meet the criteria.

- Students may have difficulty applying the terms *fewer, less than,* or *odd* in this situation.

- Students may not be able to organize their work and may become confused between the value of a coin and how many coins of each type they have.

- Students may not begin their count with the largest value.

Launch

Ask questions about the presidency: "Who can tell me the name of the president of the United States?" "Does anyone know how many presidents we have had?" "Who knows the name of the first president?" "Does anyone know any other presidents?" "Where do you see pictures of the presidents?" Display images of a penny, nickel, dime, and quarter, or give students currency manipulatives to use for the task. Ask, "Do you know the name of any of these presidents?" "What is the name of each coin?" "How much is each coin worth?" "If I have one of each coin, how much do I have all together?" Record all of the proffered information on a class poster for all to see and reference throughout the task.

Explain to students that you have $0.85 in your pocket and want to know which coin combination you might have. Share some of their results using the table format on the opposite page. Allow students to share how they counted to verify their total of $0.85. Focus students' attention on skip counting and adding the values in order from the most valued coin to the least valued coin.

Pose the following questions to check for understanding:

- How many coins with images of President Washington (or Roosevelt, Jefferson, Lincoln) do you have? How much is this worth?

- Do you have more or fewer _____ than _____?

- Do you have an odd or even number of _____?

- Do you have fewer than four dimes?

EXPLORE

Hand out the task to pairs of students and read the task aloud. Remind students which president is on each coin. As students find combinations that meet the criteria, encourage them to keep a list of the equations as a mechanism to check the reasonableness of their results. Attend to students' use of the currency symbols. Notice if students find the sum by counting coins starting with the highest value coin or in another order.

Ask these questions to check for understanding:

- Is it possible for Caleb to have five coins with the image of President Washington (quarters)? Why or why not?
- How many coins with an image of President Roosevelt (dimes) are possible? Why?
- How much is _____ dimes (or quarters, nickels, pennies) worth?
- Is there another way you can verify your total is $1.25?
- Can you find another way Caleb could have $1.25 in his pocket?
- Could you find another way if Caleb had one less dime? Why or why not?

SUMMARIZE

Ask student pairs to share their results. Write each solution using the table structure from the Problem Discussion. (Be sure to discuss any solution that does not meet the criteria.) After four or five teams have shared their results, ask students to share a strategy for finding a different solution on the basis of one already given. For example, if one solution is 3 quarters, 4 dimes, 1 nickel, and 5 pennies, ask the following questions:

- Can we exchange one of the dimes for 2 nickels (resulting in 3 quarters, 3 dimes, 3 nickels, and 5 pennies)?
- Will that still total to $1.25? (Yes.) How do you know?
- Will that meet the criteria? (No.) Why or why not? (You would have an equal number of dimes and nickels.)
- Can we exchange a dime for pennies? (Yes.) How many? (10 pennies, resulting in 3 quarters, 3 dimes, 1 nickel, and 15 pennies)
- Does this meet the criteria? (Yes.) Why or why not? (There are more dimes than nickels, and the number of pennies is fewer than 40.)
- Do you think we could exchange a nickel for some pennies and still meet the criteria? (Yes, but only if there is more than one nickel in the original solution.)
- Can you and your partner find two more solutions using this strategy?

Share some of these answers. If time permits, have students make an organized list of all seventeen possibilities as shown in the table above.

DIFFERENTIATION

- To support struggling students, provide coin manipulatives.
- To support struggling students, provide a table including several of the solutions with some of the coin numbers missing.
- To support struggling students, remove the criteria and have students generate combinations that sum to $1.25, and then check each criterion one by one.
- To support struggling students, alter the task as follows so there are only three coin types involved with a sum of $1.00:

Caleb has some coins in his pocket. He noticed that the coins he had showed images of three different presidents. He sees Presidents Lincoln, Jefferson, and Roosevelt. He counted the coins and found that he has a total of $1.00. Your task is to determine how many of each coin Caleb has in his pocket using the following clues:

Clue 1: Caleb has fewer coins that have an image of President Jefferson than coins with President Roosevelt.

Clue 2: He has an odd number of coins with an image of President Roosevelt.

Clue 3 He has fewer than 40 coins with the image of President Lincoln.

- To extend this task, students could create their own sum and series of criteria.

Valentines for Friends

Avery has five good friends in her neighborhood. For Valentine's Day, she and her friends agreed that they will exchange homemade valentines. How many valentines will they share in all? Explain why your answer makes sense. Use drawings or numbers to show your thinking.

CCSSM Standards for Mathematical Practice

Practice 2: Reason abstractly and quantitatively.

Practice 4: Model with mathematics.

CCSSM Standard for Mathematical Content

2.OA.C.4: Use addition to find the total number of objects arranged in rectangular arrays with up to 5 rows and up to 5 columns; write an equation to express the total as a sum of equal addends.

Problem Discussion

Students in second grade "work with equal groups to gain foundations for multiplication" (NGA Center and CCSSO 2010, p. 19). This problem provides an opportunity for students to explore equal groups and how the number of valentines in each group relates to repeated addition. Avery and her five friends will each distribute five valentines. This situation can be modeled by six equal groups of five valentines as well as by using a rectangular array of six rows/columns of five valentines. An equation can be used to *express the total as a sum of equal addends* (2.OA.C.4).

Beyond the array, there are multiple ways to represent the problem using manipulatives or drawings. Each representation should illustrate six equal groups with five items in each group. The six equal groups are derived from Avery and her friends—a total of six friends exchanging valentines. Each equal group contains five items because each friend will be giving valentines to five friends. An equation can model the repeated addition of the equal addends (or groups): $5 + 5 + 5 + 5 + 5 + 5 = 30$ (SMP 4). Although second-grade students are not expected to represent this equation with multiplication, they will later encounter this representation of repeated addition as $6 \times 5 = 30$.

Students both *contextualize* and *decontextualize* the quantities in this equation as they reason about the task (SMP 2). In the equation, the quantities are absent of context. However, students should be asked to consider both how the *addends* and the *number of addends* relate to the problem situation. These observations can be extended to a similar problem situation involving different numbers of friends. For example, how many valentines would be exchanged among ten children?

An interesting and predictable pattern emerges when this problem situation is extended in this way, as shown in the table below:

Number of Children	Equal Addends Equation	Multiplication Equation
2	1 + 1 = 2	2 x 1 = 2
3	2 + 2 + 2 = 6	3 x 2 = 6
4	3 + 3 + 3 + 3 = 12	4 x 3 = 12
5	4 + 4 + 4 + 4 + 4 = 20	5 x 4 = 20
6	5 + 5 + 5 + 5 + 5 + 5 = 30	6 x 5 = 30
10	9 + 9 + 9 + 9 + 9 + 9 + 9 + 9 + 9 + 9 = 90	10 x 9 = 90

Ultimately, the number of valentines for any size group can be determined by identifying the equal addend (one less than the number of children) and how many times this addend should appear in the equation (the number of children). This kind of generalization is quite advanced, but given the chance to think about this pattern, some students may recognize it.

STRATEGIES

- Students may represent the situation using manipulatives. They may use six piles of five units.
- Similarly, students may draw six equal groups of five. For example, a student may draw five dots under each of six stick figures.
- Students may create an array of six rows of five valentines or six columns of five valentines.
- Once the situation is represented, students may count the individual valentines by ones or fives. Or, they may group sets of two piles of fives into tens and count by tens.
- Students may recognize that each of the six children will need five valentines. An expression could then be derived to solve the problem: 5 + 5 + 5 + 5 + 5 + 5.
- Students may skip-count by fives.

MISCONCEPTIONS/STUDENT DIFFICULTIES

- Students may not recognize that there are six children in total who will be distributing valentines.
- Students may understand that Avery will distribute five valentines, but struggle to recognize that the other children will also be distributing valentines.
- Students may represent the children and the valentines using the same manipulative or drawing notation, and then mistakenly count them as valentines.

Launch

Begin the task by asking students whether or not they are planning to make valentines for their friends for Valentine's Day. Follow up with, "How many of you make valentines for friends who aren't in this class?" "How many do you plan to make?"

The term *each* can be a challenging vocabulary word for students. Ask, "If I told you that each of the students in this class made one valentine, what would that mean to you?" Make sure that students understand how the word *each* is understood in this situation. Follow up with questions, "How many valentines would be made altogether, if each person in this class made one valentine?" and "If I told you that each of the students in this class made two valentines, what would that mean to you?"

Prepare the students for the exploration of the task by reading it aloud to them. They may be prompted to close their eyes and imagine the situation of Avery talking with five of her neighborhood friends. Assign students a partner or to groups of three, and encourage them to make use of any materials in the classroom that might help their problem-solving processes. It may be helpful to have materials already set out for students to further encourage their use. Materials may include linking cubes, counters, candy hearts, and large pieces of paper.

Explore

As students work, circulate throughout the room and attend to their representations and solution strategies. With manipulatives and drawings, it will be helpful to ask questions that require students to think about and articulate the meaning of their representations, such as the following:

- How are you using these Unifix cubes to represent the problem?
- Why do you have Unifix cubes arranged in groups of five?
- How many groups have you made? Why does this make sense with the problem?
- I see that you have drawn five dots under each stick figure. What do these dots represent?

Additionally, ask the following questions to check for understanding of the symbolic representations:

- I see that you have written an equation that has 6 fives being added together. Why are you adding fives together?
- What do these fives represent?
- Why do you have 6 fives?

Be sure that in each case, students are able to connect the numbers in the equation back to the problem situation.

For students who are struggling to represent this problem, encourage them to pay attention to only one person from the problem, Avery. Ask, "How many valentines should Avery make for her five friends? How could you use Unifix cubes, or something else, to represent the five valentines that Avery is giving her friends?" Once Avery's five valentines are successfully represented, ask the students to think about one of Avery's friends. Naming Avery's friends can provide additional support for students who are struggling to make sense of the problem.

If they have not done so already, ask students to write an equation to represent the way they solved the problem; then have each group prepare a poster or white board that demonstrates their solution strategy.

If there is a group that quickly solves this problem, ask them to solve the problem using a different number of friends. "How many valentines would be exchanged if Avery had seven friends in her neighborhood?" Asking several groups to pursue different quantities could provide enough data so that students might be able to make a generalization about the number of addends and the value of each addend given any number of friends. This generalization could be pursued in the Summarize section of the lesson or in a future lesson.

SUMMARIZE

Prepare students to do a gallery walk to see the other groups' work on this task. Ask students to pay attention to solution strategies that involved manipulatives, drawings, and equations. Also, ask them to look for strategies of others that are similar to their own.

Allow five minutes for students to observe and think about the other groups' work. When students have returned to their seats, ask them to identify which groups used manipulatives to represent the problem situation. Highlight the solution strategies that used manipulatives, and pose the following questions to the entire class:

- What does each (manipulative) represent in this representation?
- How many groups of (manipulative) are there? Why does this make sense with this problem situation?
- How many (manipulative) are in each group? Why does this make sense?

Next, highlight the solution strategies that used drawings to represent the problem. Ask similar questions, emphasizing how the various elements of an illustration connect to the problem situation. Also ask, "How are these drawings similar to the strategies that used manipulatives?" Have students indicate how elements of the drawings correspond to elements of the manipulative representations.

Finally, ask students to reflect on any equations that were used as part of a solution process. Write one on the board: $5 + 5 + 5 + 5 + 5 + 5 = 30$. Ask students about the fives, and why there are six of them. Be sure students can tie these values to the context of the problem. Finally, ask students to share strategies for adding $5 + 5 + 5 + 5 + 5 + 5$. Record several computational strategies.

If some students have been asked to investigate different numbers of friends within the same context, these solutions may also be discussed here. It will be helpful for students to see solutions for alternative numbers of children recorded together and, perhaps, in an organized list or table (see Problem Discussion). Ask the following questions:

- What do you notice about the equations used to solve these problems with different numbers of friends?
- What if there were a total of eight children exchanging valentines?
    - o What numbers would we add together? Why does this make sense?
    - o How many of these sevens would we add together? Why does this make sense?
- Can you make a prediction about what an equation might look like if Avery had ten friends in her neighborhood?

Notice that with all of these questions, the emphasis is not on the answer but rather on looking for and extending patterns!

DIFFERENTIATION

- The number of Avery's friends in the neighborhood can be adjusted to meet students' needs.
- For students who struggle to recognize that there are six children in total in the neighborhood, a mat with six stick figures drawn on it and labeled (Avery, Friend 1, Friend 2, etc.) could be provided.
- Each group of students could be assigned a different number of children in the neighborhood. The lesson emphasis could be shifted to finding a pattern in the equations representing the problem situations.
- For students who are ready to consider how multiplication notation represents repeated addition of equal addends, this concept may be introduced. Also, these students can be encouraged to make explicit connections between each factor in the multiplication equation to the number of children in the problem.

SPRING

Spring is the time for warmer temperatures, new growth, and baby animals. It brings baseball as well as Earth Day activites. This chapter is comprised of tasks that focus on place value, addition and subtraction strategies, and geometry and measurement concepts to support students' growing mathematical knowledge.

The chapter opens with two prekindergarten tasks that allow students to enhance their abilities to reason with number. The first task asks students to use clues and apply counting and cardinality to determine how many ducklings were seen at a pond. The second, "Flowers on a Spring Day," requires students to decide how to decompose six into three addends as they place flowers into vases.

The first of the two kindergarten tasks, "Play Ball!," engages students in using manipulatives to create "buckets" of ten baseballs to determine how many total balls came in a large shipment. The last of the two kindergarten tasks asks students to sort and identify attributes of baby animal cards for a local zoo. This problem also allows students to practice counting as they compare the number of cards in each category.

The two first-grade tasks build students' number sense and geometry knowledge. In "Piglets on Kramer Farm," students are asked to use manipulatives to help place thirty piglets into pens with the same number of piglets in each. As such, this task requires students to use multiple addends of equal size to sum to thirty. For the next first-grade task, students investigate attributes of triangles as they sort shapes into categories for the "April Fools' Trick" problem.

The second-grade tasks are designed to build on students' place-value concepts. For example, students are asked to sort cans for Earth Day into groups of one hundred and ten for transport to a local recycling center. In the final problem of the chapter, students can apply strategies for addition involving three-digit numbers to determine the number of people in two different Memorial Day parades. They then use place-value concepts to compare the number of people in each parade to determine which town had more people participating in its parade.

MATERIALS FOR EACH TASK, INCLUDING HANDOUTS, ARE AVAILABLE FOR DOWNLOADING AND PRINTING ON NCTM'S WEBSITE AT NCTM.ORG/MORE4U BY ENTERING THE ACCESS CODE ON THE TITLE PAGE OF THIS BOOK.

How Many Ducklings?

One spring day, a prekindergarten class went on a field trip to the Boston Public Garden. There they spotted a mother duck and her ducklings. The ducklings swam fast and were hard to count. However, the children remembered clues about the number of ducklings.

    Clue 1: There were more than 5 ducklings.

    Clue 2: There were fewer than 9 ducklings.

    Clue 3: When the ducklings swam in pairs, every duckling had a partner.

    Clue 4: The number of ducklings started with an s sound.

How many ducklings did the class see? Draw a picture to show how many ducklings were swimming with the mother duck.

CCSSM Standards for Mathematical Practice

Practice 1: Make sense of problems and persevere in solving them.

Practice 3: Construct viable arguments and critique the reasoning of others.

CCSSM Standard for Mathematical Content

K.CC.B.4: Understand the relationship between numbers and quantities; connect counting to cardinality.

Problem Discussion

In prekindergarten, children are expected to build their abilities to "Count with understanding and recognize 'how many' in sets of objects" (NCTM 2006, p. 23). This task helps students connect counting and cardinality while simultaneously asking them to use logical reasoning. Students will need to make sense of the problem, understanding that the solution must meet all criteria (SMP 1). They may find quantities that meet some—but not all—of the clues; this will require them to persevere in their problem solving when they realize that a quantity is not correct.

A table is often used as a strategy for solving a problem involving logical reasoning. The first two clues in the problem narrow the numerical possibilities to six, seven, or eight ducklings. Some children may want to consider five and nine as possibilities; they may not be familiar with the language indicating that *more than* excludes five as a possibility and *fewer than* excludes nine. The last two clues must be considered in conjunction to determine which of the possibilities (six, seven, or eight) is the correct number of ducklings.

Only the number 6 satisfies both of the remaining clues. With six or eight ducklings swimming in pairs, every duckling would have a partner (an early introduction to doubles and even numbers); however, only six meets the additional criterion of beginning with an *s* sound.

	6	7	8
When swimming in pairs, every duckling has a partner.	X		X
The number starts with an s sound.	X	X	

In this task, students are asked to consider each of the three possibilities (six, seven, and eight ducklings) on the basis of the first two clues. For each possibility, they are asked to count and name the quantity (K.CC.B.4) and determine if it meets the criteria of the remaining clues. By demonstrating how each number does or does not fit the clues, children are laying the foundation for building a viable argument as to which number fits all the criteria (SMP 3).

The implementation of this task (see Explore) includes bags of duckling cutouts and recording sheets for the students. Prepare these in advance of the task, so that the children have concrete objects to count and with which to reason.

STRATEGIES

- Children may narrow down the possibilities to six and seven ducklings, on the basis of the beginning sound of each number name.
- Children may use a manipulative (e.g., duckling cutouts) to pair up ducklings and determine if any are left over.
- Children may determine if a quantity meets the third clue through reasoning about a different quantity of ducklings. For example, if there is a duckling left over when there are seven ducklings swimming in pairs, then there will not be any left over when there are eight ducklings swimming in pairs.
- After the number possibilities are determined, children may identify which of the remaining clues those numbers satisfy, and use that information to conclude that there are six ducklings.

MISCONCEPTIONS/STUDENT DIFFICULTIES

- Children may guess any number that begins with an s sound, such as six, seven, sixteen, seventeen, and so on.
- Children may think that five ducklings and nine ducklings are viable options on the basis of the first two clues.
- Children may struggle with the rote counting sequence, cardinality, or one-to-one correspondence, obtaining incorrect counts as a result.
- Children may choose a number that does not meet all of the problem's clues.
- Children may make a "pair" of three ducklings so that no duckling is left over.

Launch

Begin this task by reading *Make Way for Ducklings* by Robert McCloskey (1941). In this story, a mother duck leads her eight ducklings to the Boston Public Garden. Plan to pause in the reading of the story to count the number of eggs or ducklings. Model one-to-one correspondence and demonstrate that the number of eggs or ducklings is the final number name verbalized. Have volunteers point to each item as the class choral-counts.

The Launch may be used as an opportunity to learn more about the Boston Public Garden. Information is available at the following websites:

- https://www.cityofboston.gov/parks/emerald/Public_Garden.asp
- http://friendsofthepublicgarden.org/
- http://swanboats.com/

Ask the class if any of them have ever seen a mother duck with a group of ducklings. If they have, ask, "What did you notice about the ducklings?" and "How did they swim around the mother duck?" Children may have noticed the clustering of the ducklings around the mother duck and the quick movements that make them difficult to count. This is very different from the orderly ducklings in *Make Way for Ducklings*.

Read the task's scenario aloud to the children, and then read each of the clues carefully, highlighting the words in the visual display if there are emerging readers in the group. Children may immediately guess that there are eight ducklings, especially if they counted them in *Make Way for Ducklings*. Tell the class that this is a different group of ducklings, and they will need to determine how many ducklings are in this group. There may be eight, or it may be another number.

Focus the class's attention on the first two clues by reading them both aloud two more times. Write numerals from one to ten on a piece of chart paper or on a white board. Ask the class, "What does it mean when it says that there are more than five ducklings?" As the children discuss what this means, cross out any numerals that are excluded (one to five). Next, ask them, "What does it mean when it says that there are fewer than nine ducklings?" As the class discusses what this means, cross out the nine and ten. As needed, clarify the meaning of *more than* and *fewer than*.

Ask the children, "So, how many ducklings *could* there be?" At this point, children may start guessing or reasoning logically about the remaining numbers. Encourage them to share a guess with a neighbor, but let them know they will have some time to explore each of the possibilities. Remind them that there are three possibilities remaining on the basis of the first two clues: six, seven, and eight ducklings.

Explore

Tell children they will be working with a partner to determine if any of the remaining options for the number of ducklings fits the other two clues. Provide each pair with a small plastic bag with six, seven, or eight duckling cutouts. In each plastic bag include a recording card for data (i.e., the number of ducklings and responses to the other two clues). Read the recording card for the children prior to partner work, and be prepared to support their reading and recording as they work.

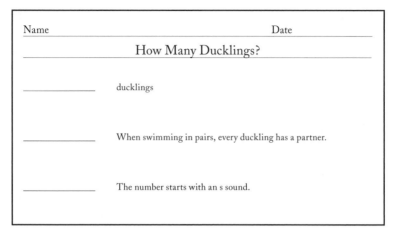

Direct partners to accomplish the following tasks using their bag of duckling cutouts:

1. Count the number of ducklings. Record this number.
2. Put ducklings in pairs to determine if any are left over.
3. Say the duckling number word to determine if it begins with an *s* sound.

For the first step, the children should be encouraged to write the numeral in the space provided on the recording card. For the last two clues, children should be directed to put a check mark if the number of ducklings matches the clue.

As children count, watch to see which children are aware that the last number verbalized is the quantity of ducklings in the set (cardinality). Also, watch for one-to-one correspondence as well as knowledge of the rote counting sequence. Children with strong correspondence and counting skills may be paired with children who may need support in one or both of these areas. Encourage both children to count to confirm their partner's result. If there is a discrepancy in their answers, ask, "Could you count the ducklings together to see if you can agree on how many there are?"

Prekindergarteners will likely use the manipulatives to make pairs of ducklings. If children struggle with this clue, ask the following questions:

- Can you show me a pair of ducklings?
- Do you think there are enough ducklings left in the bag to make another pair?
- How do you know that every duckling has a partner?
- How do you know if this number of ducklings fits this clue?

For the final clue, children may simply say the number name aloud and listen to hear the sound that it starts with. If they struggle with this task, pose a series of questions: "How many ducklings were in this bag?" "Can you say that number again for me?" "I'm going to repeat what you said, and I'd like you to listen to the first sound that you hear. What was that sound?"

As needed, assist children with writing numerals and recording their results for the bag of ducklings they are working with. When a pair finishes working with a bag, post their recording card under the appropriate number displayed during the Launch. Do not be concerned if answers are not completely correct; any discrepancies can be discussed during the Summarize period.

When a pair has finished one bag, provide them a different quantity of ducklings. Allow enough time for each pair to analyze two bags of ducklings.

SUMMARIZE

Ask students to observe the results that have been posted under the numerals 6, 7, and 8. Begin by discussing the results for seven ducklings. Questions for the group may include the following:

- Did seven ducklings fit either of the clues? Which one? Can someone demonstrate that for me?
- Which clue did not work for seven ducklings? How did you know?
- Do you see any different results on the recording cards for seven ducklings? How could you convince someone of a different answer?

As children discuss what they observed for seven ducklings, demonstrate how there is one duckling left without a partner when the ducklings swim in pairs. Also write the number name *seven* and underline the *s* at the beginning of the word, emphasizing the sound that it makes.

Next, discuss children's results for eight ducklings. Use similar questions. Again, demonstrate that every duckling has a partner when the ducklings swim in pairs. Write the number name *eight* and ask, "What letter would have to be at the beginning for this word to start with the same sound as *seven*?"

Finally, observe and discuss the results that have been posted under the numeral 6. Questions for the class may include the following:

- Can someone show me that every duckling has a partner when the ducks swim in pairs? (Demonstrate and record.)
- Can someone else convince me that six ducklings fit the other clue? (Write the number name *six*, and underline the *s*.)
- What do you think the answer to this problem is? How do you know?
- Did anyone predict that the answer was going to be six ducklings? Why did you think that number might work?

- Did anyone predict that it would be a different number of ducklings? How do we know that number does not work?

When children are confident that there are six ducklings in the group, have them paste six ducklings on a piece of paper, and write the numeral 6.

DIFFERENTIATION

- In the Launch, use another quantity of ducklings, such as four or five, to demonstrate how ducklings may be paired to swim together.
- Provide visuals for the numerals and names for numbers one to ten.
- Provide patterned sets for six, seven, and eight so children can place ducklings on top of dots in the sets. Each patterned set should be labeled with a numeral.
- To open the task to more than one possible answer, delete the last clue; therefore, six and eight could be possible solutions.
- To broaden the number of numerical possibilities, change the first two clues to the following:
    o There were more than 3 ducklings.
    o There were fewer than 10 ducklings.

FLOWERS ON A SPRING DAY

On a sunny spring day, a student picked 6 flowers. The student needs your help deciding how to put the flowers into 3 vases. How many flowers could be in each vase?

CCSSM Standard for Mathematical Practice
Practice 2: Reason abstractly and quantitatively.

Standard for Mathematical Content
According to NCTM's *Principles and Standards for School Mathematics* (2000), pre-K through grade 2 "students should develop a sense of whole numbers and represent and use them in flexible ways, including relating, composing, and decomposing numbers" (NCTM 2000, p. 78). Specifically, in prekindergarten, students "develop an understanding of the meanings of whole numbers and recognize the number of objects in small groups" (NCTM 2006, p. 11).

Problem Discussion
This task requires students to reason quantitatively to decompose the number 6 into three addends (e.g., 2 + 2 + 2 or 1 + 4 + 1; SMP 2). Students are given cutouts of six flowers and three vases and must decide how many flowers to place in each vase. They will need to use one-to-one correspondence to correctly count each flower. The task will build on students' understanding of cardinality by emphasizing the ordinal-cardinal connection (Clements and Sarama 2009); that is, students connect the rote count with the number of flowers in each vase and can answer "how many" questions about each vase and the total number of flowers.

Strategies
- Students may use manipulatives (e.g., flower cutouts) or drawings to represent the flowers in the vases.
- Students may place an equal number of flowers in each vase.
- Students may use a guess-and-check strategy. For example, they may place one flower in a vase, four in another, and see they have one left for the third vase.
- To prove there are six flowers in all, students may count all or skip-count by twos.
- Students may not fill a vase, prompting a discussion of zero.

MISCONCEPTIONS/STUDENT DIFFICULTIES

- Students may place one flower in each vase and not understand they can place more than one flower in a vase.
- Students may need to recount each time a flower is placed to determine how many flowers are in each vase and in all. For example, after placing all six flowers into the vases, students recount to see they have six flowers in all.
- Students may assume the only way to accomplish the task is to share the flowers equally among the three vases.

LAUNCH

Say, "Today I have a special number. I am going to show it to you and see if you can guess my number." Draw or show the first image below. Give students time to count the dots. Ask students to tell a neighbor what the special number is. Draw or show students the second image of the special number. Have students tell their neighbor what the special number is. Show both images and ask students to share how they counted to find the special number using each image. Display the numeral 6 for all to see.

Ask the following questions to check for understanding:

- Did the special number change?
- How do you know both images show six?
- Is there a different way to make six?

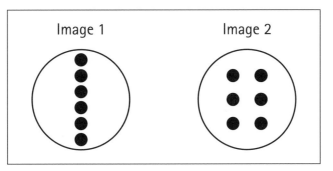

EXPLORE

Say, "Today we are going to use our special number to help a student who picked some flowers." Read the task to the students. Hand out cutouts of six flowers and three vases to each student. Ask students to count how many flowers and how many vases they have. Have students talk to an elbow partner about how they plan to place the flowers into the vases. Encourage students to find a different way from their partner's to arrange the flowers into the vases. Have students complete the task individually or in pairs. If students do not think of a way beyond an equal groups approach (i.e., two flowers in each vase), move one flower to another vase and ask if there are still six flowers in all.

Ask the following questions to check for understanding:

- How many flowers are in each vase?
- How do you know there are six flowers altogether?
- How are your vases different from your partner's?
- Can you and your partner think of another way to place the flowers in the vases?

SUMMARIZE

Ask one or more students to share their work and explain how they know there are six flowers in all. Ask if anyone else has the same picture. Ask the student(s) how they know there are six flowers in all. Now ask if anyone had a different picture and repeat the questions as before. Students may be prompted to think about zero and what this would mean in the context of the problem (e.g., one or two vases would be empty). To conclude the activity, paraphrase the different strategies students used to decompose the six flowers into three vases and prove there were six flowers in all.

DIFFERENTIATION

- To support struggling students, use only two vases.
- To extend this task, ask students to find all possible arrangements of six flowers into three vases.
- To extend this task, ask students to write the numeral on each vase that represents the number of flowers in the vase.

Play Ball!

The Lancer baseball team has a big box of baseballs, and they need your help to put them in buckets. Each bucket holds 10 baseballs. How many buckets will be needed to hold all the baseballs? How many baseballs does the team have?

CCSSM Standard for Mathematical Practice

Practice 7: Look for and make use of structure.

CCSSM Standards for Mathematical Content

K.NBT.A.1: Compose and decompose numbers from 11 to 19 into ten ones and some further ones, e.g., by using objects or drawings, and record each composition or decomposition by a drawing or equation (such as 18 = 10 + 8); understand that these numbers are composed of ten ones and one, two, three, four, five, six, seven, eight, or nine ones.

K.CC.A.1: Count to 100 by ones and by tens.

Problem Discussion

In the context of the problem, students will use strategies to compose and decompose numbers from 11 to 19 (K.NBT.A.1). They will first apply a strategy to correctly count the number of baseballs on their sheet. These strategies may include counting all, subitizing a small set, skip counting by that number, or counting on from that number. Next, students must decompose numbers between 11 to 19 using place-value concepts. For example, students must understand the structure of the base-ten number system in order to recognize 14 as one group of ten and four more ones and write the equation 14 = 10 + 4 (SMP 7). Students will also need to compose ones to make bundles of ten.

This task is designed to allow students to use manipulatives to "bundle, or group, objects into tens and count by tens" as well as "'unbundle' or 'ungroup' the tens as they decompose the quantities" (Dougherty et al 2010, p. 37). Once students create bundles of ten, they will need to "transition from viewing 'ten' as simply the accumulation of 10 ones to see it both as 10 ones and as 1 ten" (NCTM 2000, p. 33). Students who have yet to develop the concept of cardinality will have difficulty recognizing that the bundle of ten represents 10 ones without needing to recount each one. When combining groups' bundles of ten to find a total count of all the baseballs, these students may also have difficulty connecting the "skip-count by tens" chant (K.CC.A.1) to the concept that each consecutive ten represents ten more objects in the total count. For example, when students say "ten, twenty, thirty," they may not recognize that thirty represents the quantity of thirty baseballs.

Strategies

- Students may directly model the number of baseballs by using manipulatives or drawings, or use tools such as double ten-frames, to create a group of ten with some ones left over.
- Students may count all and then decompose into ten and some more (e.g., 16 = 10 + 6).
- Students may subitize and then count by twos or fives to count all.
- Students may count up to ten and determine how many ones are left over to find the total (e.g., 10 + 6 = 16).
- Students may decompose the number of balls into a group of ten and some ones.
- When composing groups of ten from the leftover ones, students may need to directly model and count all to create an additional group of ten.
- When composing groups of ten from the leftover ones, students may use manipulatives or drawings to count on from one addend to create an additional group of ten.
- When composing groups of ten from the leftover ones, students may see it as an unknown addend problem and use number partners to make ten.

Misconceptions/Student Difficulties

- Students may miscount the number of baseballs on their slip.
- Students who struggle with the conservation of cardinality may need to count by ones to verify the number of baseballs each time and not recognize that a group of ten also represents 10 ones without needing to recount each time.
- If students are using a counting-on strategy, they may have a counting error such as counting on from six baseballs by counting "six, seven, eight, nine, ten," and saying they need "five more baseballs to make ten."
- Students may confuse the number of buckets with the number of leftover baseballs.

Launch

Individually display each of the double ten-frame situations below, and ask students to identify the number represented by each.

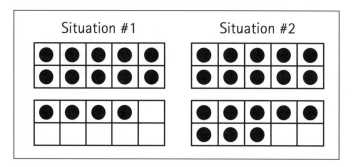

Students should share strategies for determining the number depicted. Students may count all, compose a new group of ten, skip-count by twos, fives, or tens, or use number facts to find an answer. Encourage students to use vocabulary such as *group of ten, bundle of ten,* and so on. Record an equation representing each number, for example, 14 = 10 + 4 or 18 = 10 + 8.

Ask the following questions to check for understanding:

- How many groups of five do we have? How do you know?
- How many groups of ten do we have? How do you know?
- How many ones are left over? How do you know?
- How many more ones would we need to make another group of ten?

EXPLORE

Start by saying, "Today we are going to use our make-ten strategies to help the Lancer baseball team solve a problem they have." Read the task to students. Explain to them that as a class they are going to help the team sort the baseballs into buckets and then determine how many baseballs were in the box. They and their partner will receive one of the nine slips of paper with a number (11 to 19) of baseballs from the shipment. With their partner they will need to determine how many buckets (groups of ten) are needed and how many baseballs are left over. Students will also write an equation to represent the situation.

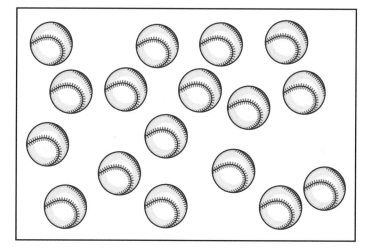

Ask the following questions to check for understanding:

- How many groups of five do you have? How do you know?
- How many groups of ten do you have? How do you know?
- How many ones are left over? How do you know?
- How many more ones would you need to make another group of ten?

Next, have student pairs form groups of four to determine how many buckets and leftover baseballs they would have by combining their baseballs. Have each group report the number of buckets and number of leftover baseballs, and display each group's numbers for the class to see. If students struggle to relate one bucket to ten baseballs, draw a bucket and mark ten dots to show the number of baseballs. Ask the groups to determine how to use this information to find how many buckets they need to store all their baseballs and how many baseballs are left over.

Ask the following questions to check for understanding:

- Do you have enough leftover baseballs to make a new group of ten? How do you know?
- Could you make one new group of ten? How do you know? How many would be left over?
- Could you make another group of ten? How do you know? How many would be left over?
- How many groups of ten could you create?
- How many baseballs are left over?

Summarize

Ask students to share strategies for determining the number of buckets and leftover baseballs. Strategies might include using double ten-frames to organize the baseballs into groups of ten, drawing a picture and circling groups of ten, or using derived number facts to make groups of ten. For example, "There are three left over from this group and seven left over from that group, so together they make one more bucket of ten baseballs."

To conclude the activity, ask students to think of a method for finding the total number of baseballs in the shipment. Have students share their plans. Focus attention on the more efficient strategy of skip counting by ten. Allow students to work with their group to use this method to verify how many baseballs were in the shipment. Because the total number of baseballs is more than one hundred, have the class skip-count out loud to find the total number of baseballs.

Differentiation

- To support struggling students, allow the use of manipulatives and double ten-frames.
- To support struggling students, when sharing each group's buckets and leftover baseballs, include pictures of each bucket with the ten baseballs represented by dots.
- The total number of baseballs in the shipment can be modified by selecting appropriate slips for each partnership.
- Extend the task by asking students to include equations for their foursome's combined total number of baseballs. For example, if the combined total is twenty-three, students write the equation $23 = 20 + 3$ or $23 = 10 + 10 + 3$.

BABY ANIMALS

A kindergarten class went to the zoo and bought some baby animal posters. The class wants to hang the posters near the door of the school. How could you sort the posters into two or more groups to hang on the wall?

CCSSM Standard for Mathematical Practice

Practice 3: Construct viable arguments and critique the reasoning of others.

CCSSM Standard for Mathematical Content

K.MD.B.3: Classify objects into given categories; count the numbers of objects in each category and sort the categories by count.

Problem Discussion

This problem requires students to sort and classify objects into two or more categories and to determine the number of objects in each category (K.MD.B.3). Through this activity, children learn to use chosen attributes to sort objects, thus laying the foundation for data analysis (NCTM 2006). When selecting collections of objects for students to sort and classify, "the best collections are those in which the objects share several attributes so they can be grouped in more than one way. This helps children create different relationships among the material and begin thinking more flexibly" (Moomaw 2011, p. 77). The animals chosen for this task can be sorted in many different ways on the basis of a variety of observable as well as unobservable attributes. The observable characteristics include but are not limited to the number of legs, the type of habitat, or the letters in the name of the animal. Unobservable traits may include modes of movement (flying, swimming, or walking), behaviors such as hours of activity (diurnal or nocturnal) or hunting (predator or prey), food consumed (carnivore, herbivore, or omnivore), and so on.

Furthermore, this task provides a context for students to practice counting and comparison skills. As they count to find the total number of posters in each category, students must pair the correct number name with each poster (K.CC.B.4.A). They also need to recognize that the last number verbalized represents the total number of posters in the category (K.CC.B.4.B) as well as write the numeral related to this count (K.CC.A.3). Students then use these counts to compare the number of posters in each category to order the categories by size. To accomplish this, "children also must understand that each counting number is quantitatively one more than the one before" (Clements and Sarama 2009, p. 46).

As part of this task students are asked to explain their choice of categories and justify why each poster is in a particular category. They also critique the reasoning of other students in regard to their choices of categories. In addition, when students order their categories by size, they must explain how they arrived at the order (SMP 3).

STRATEGIES

- Students may sort into two categories based upon observable attributes.
- Students may sort into two categories based upon unobservable attributes.
- Students may sort into three categories based upon observable or unobservable attributes.
- Students may count all to determine the number of posters in each category.
- Students may subitize or skip-count to determine the number of posters in each category.
- Students may use manipulatives that represent the count of each category in order to compare or order the categories by size.

MISCONCEPTIONS/STUDENT DIFFICULTIES

- Students may create categories that are not discrete, resulting in an animal being placed in more than one category.
- If students are using objects or drawing pictures, they may miscount the total number of objects.
- If students are using a counting-on or counting-down strategy, they may have a counting error such as counting on from six animals by counting "six, seven, eight, nine, ten," and saying they need "five more animals to make ten."

LAUNCH

To begin this task, ask students to share something they like about spring. If students do not mention the arrival of baby animals, discuss this as one sign of spring. Then ask students to think about which baby animal is their favorite. Have students talk to a neighbor about their favorite baby animal.

Display these three baby animal posters: elephant, tiger, and whale. Ask students to silently think about what is similar and different about each baby animal. Then ask students to discuss their thoughts with a neighbor. Next, ask students to share their observations with the whole class. Record a list of the attributes they used to compare and contrast the baby animals. The list of attributes may include habitat, color, number of legs, presence of fur, food consumed, and so on.

EXPLORE

Read the task aloud and hand out the fifteen posters to pairs of students. Allow the students to sort the posters into two or more categories that they choose. Encourage the students to verbalize the attribute they are using to sort the posters. Have students share their sorts with another pair to critique their reasoning. Once they have finalized their sorting, ask students to place their categories in order, from largest to smallest number of baby animals. To ensure each pair has correctly ordered their categories, ask the same pairs to explain to each other how they ordered their groups.

Ask the following questions to check for understanding:

- How did you sort your posters? What will you name your categories?
- How did you know which animals to place in each category?
- How do you know there are (number) baby animal posters in this category?
- Why did you put the categories in this order?
- Which category has the most/fewest baby animal posters? How do you know?

SUMMARIZE

Have each student pair glue the posters on a large piece of construction paper, separating the categories by drawing lines, and then identifying each category and writing the total number of posters for each. Model this by showing students where you would like them to place the category name and total on their paper. Students can then present their posters to the class.

Ask the following questions to check for understanding:

- When groups share their categories, ask, "How do you know each of those animals belong to that category?"

- This team's largest/smallest category had (number) posters. Does anyone have a category with more/fewer than (number) posters?

- Did anyone have the same number of posters in each of their categories?

- How many more posters are needed in this category to make the categories the same size? How do you know?

To conclude, ask students to think of one baby animal they could add to their largest/smallest category.

DIFFERENTIATION

- To support students who struggle to identify categories, have them use an attribute from the list generated in the Launch.
- To support students who struggle, decrease the number of posters.

- To support students who struggle to compare and order the categories by size, allow them to use linking cubes to represent the quantities and directly compare the linking cube towers to order the categories.

- To extend this task, ask students to write an equation to represent their addends that sum to fifteen.

- To extend this task, ask students to create additional baby animal posters to add to each of their categories.

- To extend this task, after student pairs sort their posters have them trade with another pair. Then ask students to identify the attributes on which the sorts were based.

PIGLETS ON KRAMER FARM

This spring, 30 piglets were born on Kramer Farm. The farm needs to make pens for the 30 piglets. Each pen needs to hold the same number of piglets. Will you help Kramer Farm find all the ways it can pen the 30 piglets so there is the same number of piglets in each pen?

CCSSM STANDARD FOR MATHEMATICAL PRACTICE

Practice 8: Look for and express regularity in repeated reasoning.

CCSSM STANDARD FOR MATHEMATICAL CONTENT

1.OA.A.2: Solve word problems that call for addition of three whole numbers whose sum is less than or equal to 20, e.g., by using objects, drawings, and equations with a symbol for the unknown number to represent the problem.

PROBLEM DISCUSSION

Students in first grade are expected to solve word problems involving three addends whose sum is within twenty (1.OA.A.2). The focus of this task is on the use of drawings or manipulatives to solve a put-together/take-apart problem that requires students to find sums of thirty using multiple addends of equal size. In preschool and kindergarten, students begin to solve problems related to the four operations. However, "their strategies are not as sophisticated as those of older children; nevertheless, like all mathematicians, young children apply the foundational knowledge that they have already developed to more challenging and interesting problems" (Moomaw 2011, p. 46).

This task provides the opportunity for students to grapple with the idea of equal groups as repeated addition; for example, students may recognize thirty as 10 + 10 + 10 and place ten piglets into three pens. Knowing there are thirty piglets to place in pens, some students may use a sharing approach, that is, they select the number of pens and share the piglets one at a time into the pens until they run out of piglets or have leftovers. Both of these strategies promote the development of number sense and eventually lead to working with equal groups as a foundation for multiplication and division in later grades (NCTM 2000). When solving this task, students may use repeated reasoning as they notice their solution can lead to another solution (SMP 8). For example, students may notice that they can split the ten piglets in three pens into five piglets in six pens. They may then use the same shortcut to realize that ten pens of three piglets can easily be rearranged to make five pens of six piglets.

STRATEGIES

- Students may use a trial-and-error strategy to make piles and count all to check that there are an equal number in each pile.

- Students may guess a number of piglets for each pen and use an equal groups/ repeated addition strategy to determine the number of pens. For example, students may choose five piglets for each pen and create groups of five until they run out of piglets, or decide on four piglets for each pen and then realize they have piglets left over and change their decision.

- Students may guess a number of pens and use a sharing strategy to determine the number of piglets in each pen. For example, students may decide on five pens and share the piglets one at a time until they run out of piglets, and then check to see that each pen has an equal number of piglets.

- Once students find one arrangement of pens and piglets, they may recognize they can reverse the quantities to find a second solution; for example, six pens of five piglets would become five pens of six piglets.

- Once students find one arrangement of pens and piglets, they may build on their strategy to find another solution. For example, once students determine three pens with ten piglets in each pen, they may break apart their groups of ten into groups of five and notice there are six equal groups of five piglets.

- To check the reasonableness of their results, students may count all piglets in each group to verify they have equal groups in every pen.

- To check the reasonableness of their results, students may skip-count the number of piglets in each group to verify they have thirty piglets in all.

Misconceptions/Student Difficulties

- Students may attempt a repeated-addition or equal-groups strategy, but struggle to understand what to do with the leftover piglets when the chosen number is not a divisor of thirty.

- Students may select a number of pens and share the piglets one by one into these pens, but fail to check that there are an equal number of piglets in each pen.

- Students may not find all the ways to arrange the piglets into pens because they do not recognize that the number of piglets and pens can be reversed to find a different solution.

Launch

Ask students if they have ever been on a farm and what animals they saw or might see at a farm. Tell students that you saw twenty baby chicks at a farm. The chicks were in groups eating corn. Ask students to find different ways to show how the twenty chickens may have been in groups. Have students write a number sentence to represent their thinking. Encourage students to use more than two addends if they do not do so on their own. Have students share with the class their number sentences and how they know their addends (groups) sum to twenty. Highlight those that use equal addends or skip-counting methods (e.g., 10 + 10 or 5 + 5 + 5 + 5).

EXPLORE

Have students work with a partner to complete the task. Hand out thirty manipulatives to each pair. Read the task to students, highlighting the fact that there should be an equal number of piglets in each pen.

Ask the following questions to check for understanding:

- What do you think would be a good number for the amount of piglets in each pen? Can you make piles of that number? Are there any piglets left over? How do you know?
- What do you think would be a good number of pens? Can you put the piglets in the pens so there is the same number in each pen? Are there the same number in each pen? How do you know?
- How do you know your solution is correct?
- Can you find another solution?

SUMMARIZE

Ask students to share their solutions with another pair. Then have students report to the entire class how they found the number of piglets and pens. (See the possible strategies listed above.) Record their solutions using a picture of each pen with the number of piglets represented by dots, such as the example below of five pens with six piglets in each.

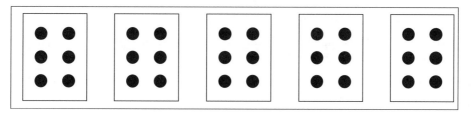

Keep a list indicating the number of pens and piglets like the one below:

1 pen of 30 piglets
2 pens of 15 piglets
3 pens of 10 piglets
5 pens of 6 piglets
6 pens of 5 piglets
10 pens of 3 piglets
15 pens of 2 piglets
30 pens of 1 piglet

After recording the picture, ask the pair to explain how they know how many dots are in each pen. Students may count all or use subitizing. Then, ask the students to describe how they know this represents thirty piglets. Strategies may include counting all, counting on, skip counting, or using number facts such as doubles or anchoring to ten. Repeat this process until all possible solutions have been identified. In the event that not all solutions have been recognized, ask questions such as, "Could Kramer Farm have one pen for all thirty piglets?" or "Could Kramer Farm have pens with just two piglets in each pen?"

Once all solutions have been listed, ask students to discuss with their partner what they notice about the list of solutions. Students should recognize that the number of piglets and pens could be reversed and still result in thirty total piglets. Also, students may observe that in some cases when the number of pens is doubled, the number of piglets in each pen is halved. For example, this is the case with the solutions of three pens of ten piglets and six pens of five piglets.

To conclude this activity, ask students to decide which of the solutions they think is the best for the Kramer Farm piglets. This question allows students to link the task with practical issues such as cost of materials to build multiple pens and how crowded a pen may be.

DIFFERENTIATION

- To support struggling students, decrease the number of piglets to twenty so they can build on ideas shared during the launch.
- To support struggling students, ask them for two solutions instead of all solutions.
- To extend this task, ask students questions such as the following:
    o If there were twenty piglets on Kramer Farm, would there be more or fewer solutions than for thirty piglets?
    o If there were forty piglets on Kramer Farm, would there be more or fewer solutions than for thirty piglets?
    o Students could also choose their own number of piglets and determine the solutions for their chosen number.

April Fools' Trick

The first-grade class went on a field trip to a local bakery. The baker was planning to make cookies in the shape of triangles for the students. When the baker opened the drawer of triangle cookie cutters, he discovered that someone had played an April Fools' trick on him. The drawer had cookie cutters that were triangles and cookie cutters that were not triangles. Will you help the baker decide which cookie cutters are triangles and which are not?

CCSSM Standard for Mathematical Practice

Practice 6: Attend to precision.

CCSSM Standard for Mathematical Content

1.G.A.1: Distinguish between defining attributes (e.g., triangles are closed and three-sided) versus nondefining attributes (e.g., color, orientation, overall size); build and draw shapes to possess defining attributes.

Problem Discussion

This task engages students in discourse in order to define attributes of triangles and to distinguish between triangles and nontriangles (1.G.A.1). Kindergarten students are expected to be able to recognize several two-dimensional shapes (squares, circles, triangles, and rectangles), regardless of their orientation or size (K.G.A.2). The van Hiele levels describe stages of geometric reasoning through which students progress. Children transition from the visual level, "It's a triangle because it's pointy," to the descriptive level, "It's a triangle because it has three straight sides" (Moomaw 2011).

To promote the transition from the visual to the descriptive level, students need opportunities to engage with "varied examples and nonexamples, discussions about shapes and their attributes, a wider variety of shape classes and a broad array of shape tasks. … This is especially important for classes that have more diverse examples, such as triangles" (Clements and Sarama 2009, p. 133). Throughout this task, students must decide upon and communicate precisely the defining attributes (SMP 6) of triangles using age-appropriate language. Through discussion, students will develop a more robust definition of a triangle, which includes attributes such as *closed* and *three straight sides* (which results in *three pointed corners or vertices*). In later grades, these attributes will lead to a definition of a triangle as a *polygon with three sides*.

Strategies

- Students may recognize the rectangle and semicircle as nonexamples.
- Students may first identify triangles that "look like" equilateral triangles; that is, they include triangle-like shapes with slightly rounded vertices (shape L, following page) or slightly curved sides (shapes C and I, following page).

- Students may count the number of sides or "lines" and identify all shapes with three sides as triangles.
- Students may attend to precision and identify only shapes that have three straight sides and three pointed vertices, excluding the obtuse triangles (shapes B and K, right).
- Students may attend to precision and identify only shapes that have three straight sides and three pointed vertices (shapes A, B, F, H, J and K, right).

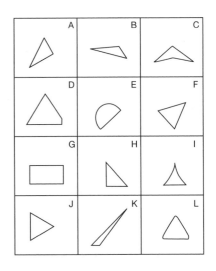

MISCONCEPTIONS/STUDENT DIFFICULTIES

- Students do not attend to precision and focus simply on three sides (whether they are straight or curved) and corners (whether they are pointed or rounded) as opposed to the more precise attributes of three straight sides and three pointed vertices.
- Students may focus on orientation and exclude those triangles that do not have a side parallel to the bottom of the cutout.
- Students may not recognize the obtuse triangles as satisfying the attributes of a triangle because they look so different from the typical triangles they have experienced.

LAUNCH

To encourage students to verbalize attributes of shapes, display the rectangle and the irregular shape (actual cookie cutters can also serve this purpose) directly below. Ask students to discuss with a partner how the shapes are similar and how they are different. Have a few students share their ideas with the class. Focus students' attention on specific, precise attributes; for example, if a student says the rectangle has four sides, ask students to clarify how the sides are different from those in the irregular shape. Next, have students compare and contrast the irregular shape and the circle. The circle may be difficult for children to describe. The goal is to have students contrast the two straight sides of the irregular shape and the roundness of the circle.

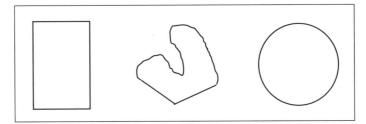

EXPLORE

Prior to class, cut apart the rectangular regions, not the shapes. It is important that the shapes remain within the rectangles so students can grapple with orientation. Read the task to students. Hand out sets of the shapes to each pair of students. Have students sort the shapes representing the cookie cutters into two piles: those that are triangles and those that are not.

Ask the following questions to check for understanding:

- Why did you place that shape in the triangle (or nontriangle) group?
- Why didn't you place this shape in the triangle (or nontriangle) group?
- Point at two shapes in the triangle group and ask, "How are these shapes the same and how are they different?"
- Can you tell me how you decided which pile this shape belongs in?

After partners have completed their sort, ask them to join another pair to justify their choices and come to a consensus regarding which shapes are triangles and which are not. Focus students' attention on the attributes of each shape and on which attributes are necessary for a shape to be labeled a triangle.

SUMMARIZE

Create a T-chart large enough for all students to see. Hold up each shape and ask students if the shape is a triangle or not. If all the students agree on the shape's type, place that shape on the T-chart in the corresponding column. Each time, have students justify why or why not the shape is a triangle. If students do not all agree on the placement of a shape, set that one aside until all the shapes have been displayed, and then discuss those shapes that did not receive consensus. Ask questions to focus attention on defining attributes, such as "Does the shape have three straight sides?" or "Could we create this shape using three pieces of uncooked spaghetti?"

To conclude the activity, ask students to write a note with their partners to the baker describing how to decide if a cookie cutter is a triangle or not. They could also be asked to include examples of triangle cookie cutters for the baker.

DIFFERENTIATION

- To accommodate struggling students, remove the variants (shapes B and K).
- To accommodate struggling students, remove the difficult distractors (shapes C, D, I, and L) and replace them with known nontriangular shapes.
- To extend this task, ask students to create their own April Fools' cookie-cutter sort for rectangles.

Recycling Cans for Earth Day

The second-grade class at Emerson Elementary collected cans for Earth Day. They can be turned in to the recycling center in trash bags that hold 100 cans and grocery bags that hold 10 cans. The second-grade class collected a total of 372 cans. What are different ways the students can sort the cans into bags to take to the recycling center? Choose which way you think is best and write a letter to Emerson Elementary describing why your method is the best method.

CCSSM Standard for Mathematical Practice

Practice 7: Look for and make use of structure.

CCSSM Standard for Mathematical Content

2.NBT.A.1: Understand that the three digits of a three-digit number represent amounts of hundreds, tens, and ones; e.g., 706 equals 7 hundreds, 0 tens, and 6 ones.

Problem Discussion

This task builds on students' first-grade experiences in which they developed place-value understanding for two-digit numbers (1.NBT.B.2) and connected the number words, numerals, and quantities to these two-digit numbers (Clements and Sarama 2009). That is, first-grade students come to an understanding that thirty-five is represented as the numeral 35 and not 305 and that it can be represented as 30 + 5 or as 10 + 10 + 10 + 5 (three groups of ten and five ones). In second grade, students extend this understanding to three-digit numbers (2.NBT.A.1). This task explores the place-value concept "that all adjacent places have the same exchange values: exchange one unit to the left for ten units to the right and vice versa" (Clements and Sarama 2009, p. 89).

Students are asked to find multiple representations of the number 372 using groups of hundreds, tens, and ones. They will need to recognize the base-ten structure of the number system as they compose groups of 10 tens or 10 ones and decompose a group of 1 hundred or 1 ten into 10 tens or 10 ones, respectively (SMP 7). Through the context of the problem, students are able to make decisions about the reasonableness of three large trash bags, which they may not be able to carry, versus thirty-seven small grocery bags, which may take more trips, but are easier to carry. Students will also need to consider the practicality of breaking apart a bag of ten cans and two leftovers into twelve leftover cans. Students may use a variety of strategies to verify the number of cans they have, including skip counting by place value and combining place-value parts (Battista 2012).

Strategies

- Students may decompose the 7 grocery bags and 2 leftovers into 6 grocery bags and 12 leftovers.

- Students use their knowledge of the expanded form of the number (300 + 70 + 2) to find the solution of 3 trash bags, 7 grocery bags, and 2 leftovers.

- Students may take away 10 cans from 300 to create an additional grocery bag, and then repeat this process, keeping track of how many times they have created a grocery bag, until they have 2 trash bags, 17 grocery bags, and 2 leftovers.

- Students may automatically decompose one trash bag of 100 cans into 10 grocery bags with 10 cans in each bag.

- When asked how many cans in all, students may skip-count by place value. For example, 2 trash bags, 17 grocery bags, and 2 leftovers are counted as "100, 200, 210, 220, … 370, 371, 372."

- When asked how many cans in all, students may combine place-value parts such as grouping 5 grocery bags together and knowing this represents 50 cans without counting by tens. For example, 2 trash bags, 17 grocery bags, and 2 leftovers is the same as 2 trash bags, 5 + 5 + 5 + 2 grocery bags, and 2 leftovers and counted as "200, 250, 300, 350, 370, 372."

- When asked how many cans in all, students may use a number sentence to find the total number of cans; for example, the sum of 2 trash bags, 17 grocery bags, and 2 leftovers is found by 200 + 170 + 2.

MISCONCEPTIONS/STUDENT DIFFICULTIES

- Students may not understand how to exchange adjacent place values; for instance, one group of 100 can be exchanged for ten groups of 10.

- Students may only focus on the digits that represent the number of bags and not remember what the bags represent (e.g., 3 trash bags represent 3 cans, not 300 cans.)

- If students focus on the number of each size bag rather than how many cans are represented by the number, they may notice that 3, 7, and 2 sum to 12 and find the solution 2, 8, 2.

- Students may think the number of each type of bag leads directly to the written numeral that represents the total number of cans; for example, 2 trash bags, 17 grocery bags, and 2 leftovers are represented as 2,172.

LAUNCH

Ask students to think about how many cans are recycled every second in the United States. Have students participate in a four-corners activity where they choose the range of numbers that represents their guess. Corners could be labeled less than 100, between 100 and 1,000, between 1,000 and 3,000, more than 3,000. According to the Can Manufacturers Institute website (www.cancentral.com), 105,800 cans are recycled each minute in the United States, at approximately 1,763 cans per second.

Write the number 1,763 on the board. Ask students to discuss with a classmate in their corner what each of the digits in the number represents; for example, two students might discuss that the 7 represents seven groups of 100 or 700 cans. Finally, have students share with the larger group.

EXPLORE

Distribute the handout and read the task as a class. Clarify that the trash bags hold 100 cans and that the grocery bags hold 10 cans. Showing a trash bag and a grocery bag to students may help them better understand the context. Ask students to individually find two ways to organize the 372 cans into bags. For students who are struggling to decompose 100 into ten groups of 10, provide base-ten manipulatives. Have them record their work in the table on their handout. Students should then work with a partner to prove that each of their solutions does indeed total 372 cans.

Ask the following questions to check for understanding:

- What does the (number) mean in the trash bag (or grocery bag or leftovers) column? (You are seeking an answer that includes the number of cans in each bag and the total number of cans. For example, the 3 in the trash bag column means 3 bags each with 100 cans for a total of 300 cans.)
- How many groups of ten are in 170? How do you know?
- How did you decompose the number of cans in the trash bag? (Did they repeatedly take 10 away from 100 or did they automatically know 100 could be decomposed into ten groups of 10?)
- How do you know you have 372 cans? Can you count the total number of cans in a different way? (Do they skip-count by place value or combine place-value parts?)
- Is it possible to have more than 2 cans leftover? Why or why not?

SUMMARIZE

Select a student to fill in one line of the table and share his strategy for proving his numbers represent 372 cans. Ask students who had the same answer if they have another method for proving this entry represents 372 cans. Then ask if anyone has a different solution, repeating the process until all possible entries with no more than 2 leftover cans are entered into the table. Placing their solutions as ordered in the table below allows students to investigate the structure of place value in the task. For example, they may notice that when the number of trash bags goes down by one, the number of garbage bags increases by ten. The solutions in the table are those that contain the fewest number of leftovers. Students may find solutions that do not minimize the number of leftovers, such as 3 trash bags (300 cans), 5 grocery bags (50 cans), and 22 leftover cans.

Encourage a variety of strategies, including skip counting by place value and combining place-value parts. For the solution of 2 trash bags, 17 grocery bags, and 2 leftovers, a student may count "100, 200, 210, 220, … 370, 371, 372." For the same solution a student who combines place-value parts may count "200, 250, 300, 350, 370, 372." If students use a number sentence such as "The total of 2 trash bags, 17 grocery bags, and 2 leftovers is found by 200 + 170 + 2," include it in a fourth column. If a student has decomposed a group of ten into 10 ones, discuss the practicality of the solution in the context of the problem.

Trash Bag	Grocery Bag	Leftover Cans
3	7	2
2	17	2
1	27	2
0	37	2

DIFFERENTIATION

- To support struggling students, encourage the use of base-ten manipulatives.
- To accommodate struggling students, use a smaller number, such as 145, for the number of cans to be recycled.
- To extend this task, ask students to write a number sentence for each entry in the table; for example, 1 trash bag, 27 grocery bags, and 2 leftovers can be expressed as 100 + 270 + 2.
- To extend this task, ask students to find different ways to transport 1,763 cans to the recycling center.
- To extend this task, ask students to predict how much a trash bag of 100 empty soda cans would weigh. (An empty 12-ounce soda can weighs approximately 0.5 ounce.)

MEMORIAL DAY PARADE

Two towns are planning their parades in celebration of Memorial Day.

- The town of Liberty, Oklahoma, will have 247 veterans, 214 band members, and 156 members of local groups marching in the parade.
- The town of Justice, Oklahoma, will have 258 veterans, 242 band members, and 113 members of local groups marching in the parade.

Which town, Liberty or Justice, will have more people in the parade? How many more? Explain how you know.

CCSSM STANDARDS FOR MATHEMATICAL PRACTICE

Practice 5: Use appropriate tools strategically.

Practice 7: Look for and make use of structure.

CCSSM STANDARDS FOR MATHEMATICAL CONTENT

2.NBT.A.4: Compare two three-digit numbers based on meanings of the hundreds, tens, and ones digits, using >, =, and < symbols to record the results of comparisons.

2.NBT.B.7: Add and subtract within 1000, using concrete models or drawings and strategies based on place value, properties of operations, and/or the relationship between addition and subtraction; relate the strategy to a written method. Understand that in adding or subtracting three-digit numbers, one adds or subtracts hundreds and hundreds, tens and tens, ones and ones, and sometimes it is necessary to compose or decompose tens or hundreds.

PROBLEM DISCUSSION

Although this task appears to involve straightforward addition of three-digit numbers, comparison of the sums, and finding the difference between the sums, there are actually sophisticated ways to tackle this task without pursuing these particular computations. In the *Common Core State Standards for Mathematics*, fluency with algorithms for addition and subtraction within 1000 is not expected until third grade, so this problem should be viewed as one that could be approached in multiple ways by reasoning about the place-value components of the numbers or the relative size of the groups.

For each of the towns, the 3 three-digit numbers can be modeled using base-ten blocks. These blocks can then be used to combine the three values based on place value, composing tens and hundreds as needed (2.NBT.B.7):

Liberty

247 + 214 + 156

$$= (200 + 40 + 7) + (200 + 10 + 4) + (100 + 50 + 6)$$
$$= 200 + 200 + 100 + 40 + 10 + 50 + 7 + 4 + 6$$
$$= 500 + 100 + 17$$
$$= 617 \text{ people marching in the parade}$$

Justice

258 + 242 + 113

$$= (200 + 50 + 8) + (200 + 40 + 2) + (100 + 10 + 3)$$
$$= 200 + 200 + 100 + 50 + 40 + 10 + 8 + 2 + 3$$
$$= 500 + 100 + 13$$
$$= 613 \text{ people marching in the parade}$$

For both towns, composing 1 hundred of 10 tens and 1 ten of 10 ones is a potential strategy. These sums can then be used to determine that Liberty will not only have more people marching in the parade, 617 > 613 (2.NBT.A.4) but there will also be four more people marching in Liberty. Students may choose to compose their numbers in different ways; for example, students may recognize that 58 of Justice's veterans and 42 of Justice's band members could be combined to make 100.

Modeling with base-ten blocks or careful consideration of the values in the problem may lead to a strategy in which the number of hundreds (5 hundreds for each town) and the number of tens (10 tens for each town) are excluded from the comparison because these quantities are equivalent, leaving a more efficient comparison of the ones (17 > 13). Note that comparison of the quantities in this way demonstrates early algebraic reasoning based on the structure of the numbers that are being used in the problem (SMP 7).

The quantities for the two towns may also be compared by analyzing the individual groups. The table below identifies the difference between the three categories of people marching in the parade for each town.

	Liberty	Justice	Difference
Veterans	247	258	Justice has 11 more
Band Members	214	242	Justice has 28 more
Members of Local Groups	156	113	Liberty has 43 more

Comparison of the differences between the groups reveals that Justice has a total of 39 more people marching in the parade in the veterans and band categories. However, Liberty has 43 more members of local groups marching in the parade, which means that Liberty will have 4 more people marching in its parade.

Given that students may utilize very different strategies, this task should provide ample opportunities for students to explain and justify their reasoning as well as to make sense of and critique the reasoning of others (SMP 3).

STRATEGIES

- Students may directly model the quantities in this problem (e.g., using base-ten blocks), using the model to find the sums for each parade, the comparison, and the difference between the parades.
- Students may break the quantities apart by place value and use partial sums to find the total number of people marching in each parade.
- Students may use an open number line or another tool to add the quantities together and compare the two sums.
- Students may use a model or place-value knowledge to remove quantities that are irrelevant to the comparison (i.e., the 5 hundreds and 10 tens), and then compare the remaining quantities.
- Students may compare the values in each category, identifying which town has more marchers for a category and how many more. These differences are then compared to determine the town with more people marching in the parade and the difference between the two parades.

MISCONCEPTIONS/STUDENT DIFFICULTIES

- Students may assume that because Justice has more members in two of the three categories, this town will have more people marching in the parade.
- Students may struggle with composing 10 tens to make 1 hundred, or composing 10 ones to make 1 ten.
- Students may make common addition or subtraction errors, either with facts or with algorithms.

LAUNCH

Ask students what they know about the Memorial Day holiday. Discuss the holiday and what the holiday means to Americans. Ask students how towns usually acknowledge the holiday other than by giving everyone a day off from school or work. Discuss how town parades honor the men and women who have died in service of the armed forces. Ask students whom they typically see marching in parades.

Display the Memorial Day handout to the students and read the problem aloud. Ask students what they know about the problem. Then have students turn to an elbow partner and in their own words, state what the problem is asking. Tell students to consider any tools they think might be helpful for their problem solving. Have them share their thoughts about these tools so they can be made available during the Explore portion of the lesson.

EXPLORE

Assign students to partners or groups of three. Ask them to think about a plan for solving the problem before they dig in. Provide base-ten blocks and any other materials that might be useful for their problem solving.

As students work, circulate throughout the room, identifying and recording the different strategies that are being used. Ask the following questions to assess students' understanding:

- How are you using the base-ten blocks?
- I see that you are adding the numbers together. Can you explain why you decided to use addition?
- Did you have to regroup to find the sums? How did you regroup when you added the quantities from each town?
- Why did you think it was safe to ignore some of the quantities for each of the towns?
- Which town has more veterans (or band members or local groups) marching? How many more?
- How did you find the difference between the two quantities? What does this difference tell you about the parades in Liberty and Justice?

Be sure each group of students is able to connect their reasoning and quantities to the context of the problem.

For groups that are adding the quantities for each town in order to find the total number of people in each parade, questions may direct them to recognize some similarities between the numbers. For example, "What do you notice about the hundreds blocks (flats) and the tens blocks (longs) that you have put in the two piles?" or "Do you recognize any similarities between the numbers for Liberty and the numbers for Justice?" Encourage them to think about how they might use these similarities to their advantage in solving the problem. If they have found a solution by finding the sum for each town, ask, "Do you think there is another way to do this problem where you don't have to find the total number of people marching in each parade?"

With a few minutes left before the class discussion of the problem, ask students to be sure that everyone is clear on their group's solution and reasoning so they are all able to represent the group's thinking in the class discussion.

SUMMARIZE

First, ask a group that modeled the problem using base-ten blocks to demonstrate their solution strategy. When they have finished, ask students in the audience to explain how this group used the base-ten blocks and how the blocks connected to the task. Make sure that students are clear on how the blocks were used to represent six different quantities and where they see these quantities in the problem itself. If blocks have been removed during the discussion, reposition them so the three quantities for each town are displayed for the remainder of the discussion. Use them as a reference throughout the discussion, especially with groups who have utilized more abstract reasoning.

Continue the conversation by having other groups share unique problem-solving strategies. As each group presents, ask if there are others who did the same thing. Provide them the opportunity to contribute to the discussion with questions such as "Is there anything you'd like to add about this strategy?"

The order of the strategies presented is flexible. However, if there are strategies that were noticed during the Explore section that are similar to each other (e.g., students removing the hundreds from the comparison or students removing both the hundreds and the tens from the comparison), then try to have these presented one after the other. This allows students to make sense of one strategy using another and to identify similarities and differences between the methods.

For each strategy presented, ask students to process some or all of the following questions:

- How does this strategy connect to the base-ten blocks that we have displayed?
- How did this group know which town would have more people marching in the parade?
- How did this group identify how many more people would be marching in Liberty's parade?

Questions that might be specific to strategies include the following:

- This group decided to ignore the hundreds and tens in all of the quantities. Is that safe to do? Why?
- Justice had two categories that would have more people marching than Liberty. How is it possible that Liberty is actually the one with more people in the parade?
- This group decided to combine hundreds, tens, and ones separately. How does this connect to what the other group did with the blocks?

Throughout the student presentations, encourage students in the audience to ask their own clarifying questions or to explain to their neighbors how the strategy works. Allow as much of the conversation as possible to happen between students so they get ample opportunity to defend their own reasoning as well as question others' strategies.

DIFFERENTIATION

- For students who are struggling with three-digit numbers, the hundreds digit can be removed from each of the quantities.
- If students have difficulty working with three addends for each town, remove the local groups category from the problem.
- If students make computation errors, require that they justify their reasoning with base-ten blocks.
- For students who have solved the problem quickly by adding the three quantities for each town, comparing the sums, and finding the difference, ask them to see if there is a way to solve the problem without finding the total number of people marching in each parade.

- To extend the task, ask students to change one number in the problem to make the number of people marching in each parade equal.
- To extend the task, ask students to add a category of people who might march in each parade with numbers that would shift the result to Justice by four people.

Summer

Summer is a time for outdoor activities, such as picking flowers, going to the beach, or taking a camping trip. Baseball season is in full swing, and many students are excited about summer vacation. This chapter offers tasks related to geometry that entail the sorting of shapes on the basis of defining attributes and grappling with the notion of fractional parts of a whole. Other tasks include measurement concepts, such as telling time and using money at a lemonade stand. Finally, students will employ a variety of strategies for addition and subtraction in contexts related to the summer season.

In the first task, "Summer Flowers," pre-K students are asked to sort flowers into baskets on the basis of attributes such as the number, shape, or size of the petals on each flower. The "Sand Castles" task provides students the opportunity to explore three-dimensional shapes and how they relate to two-dimensional footprints and to practice the academic vocabulary related to these concepts.

The first kindergarten task, "Sidewalk Chalk Shapes," also gives students an occasion to use academic vocabulary related to two-dimensional shapes as they identify and create shapes. In "A Weekend Camping Trip," students are asked to decompose the number 12 in order to determine how many ways twelve campers can be arranged into tents.

Telling and writing time on both analog and digital clocks is the focus of the first-grade task, "July 4th Celebration." Students are asked to explore the notion of elapsed time by comparing the length of two different parades. In the other first-grade problem, "Baseball Ticket Sales," students use clues to determine the number of tickets sold in each of four sections of a baseball stadium using a variety of addition and subtraction strategies.

"Swimming at Swan Lake" has second-grade students sorting beach towels on the basis of recognizing halves and fourths; it focuses on the notion that equal shares of identical wholes do not need to be the same shape. In the final task for second graders, "Lemonade Stand," students work with coins and their values to determine a variety of ways to spend $1.50 to purchase items costing 50¢, 25¢, and 10¢.

MATERIALS FOR EACH TASK, INCLUDING HANDOUTS, ARE AVAILABLE FOR DOWNLOADING AND PRINTING ON NCTM'S WEBSITE AT NCTM.ORG/MORE4U BY ENTERING THE ACCESS CODE ON THE TITLE PAGE OF THIS BOOK.

Summer Flowers

Children in Mrs. Shanklin's room went on a walk. They picked many flowers to place in baskets. Will you help them sort the flowers into 2 baskets so the flowers in each basket are the same in some way?

CCSSM Standard for Mathematical Practice

Practice 7: Look for and make use of structure.

CCSSM Standard for Mathematical Content

K.MD.B.3: Classify objects into given categories; count the numbers of objects in each category and sort the categories by count.

Problem Discussion

This task helps students develop logical reasoning by sorting flowers on the basis of observed attributes, such as the number of petals, number of leaves on the stem, or shape of the flower. This type of sorting activity promotes "analytical thinking and clear communication" (Moomaw 2011, p. 73). Students must sort the collection of flowers into two distinct categories on the basis of the structures they observe (SMP 7), such as the shape or size of the flower or the number of petals, flowers, or leaves on the stem. Students will practice counting skills, such as one-to-one correspondence and cardinality, as they decide which flowers fit into specific categories. One-to-one correspondence requires two distinct actions: "The counter must link each word said in *time* to one object in *space*, usually by touching or pointing to each object as each word is said" (Fuson, Clements, and Beckmann 2010, p. 13).

Furthermore, this task provides a context for students to practice comparison skills. During the Explore phase of the lesson, students are asked to determine the total number of flowers in each basket (K.MD.B.3). They are also asked to decide which basket has more or fewer flowers. Prekindergarten students may use counting and matching strategies to determine which basket has more and may begin to use words like *less* and *fewer* (Fuson, Clements, and Beckmann 2010).

Strategies

- Students may sort based upon the shape of the flowers' parts (e.g., pointed or round petals).
- Students may sort based upon the size of the flower (e.g., short or tall, fat or skinny).
- Students may sort based upon the number of petals or leaves on the stem.

Misconceptions/Student Difficulties

- Students may not know the counting sequence for those flowers with a large number of petals.
- Students may miscount the number of petals, leaves, or flowers (e.g., skipping or double counting an item).
- Students may not understand that each successive number represents a quantity that is one larger than the previous number.
- Students may have difficulty keeping track of the petals they have counted due to the circular nature of the shapes of some flowers.
- Students may be able to define one category but not another. For example, they may define one category as "have two leaves" but struggle to name the other category as "do not have two leaves."

Launch

Explain to students that today they will be looking at different types of flowers. Show students pictures of flowers from books or the Internet or bring in actual flowers. Ask students to identify the different parts of a flower, such as petal, stem, and leaves. Hand out the two large flower cutouts to each pair of students and ask students to each color one of the flowers. After they have colored the flowers, ask students to talk to their partner about how their flowers are similar and how they are different.

Ask the following questions to check for understanding:

- How many petals (leaves) does your flower have? How do you know? Can you show me how you counted the petals (leaves)?
- Which flower has more petals (leaves)? How do you know?
- How are the petals (leaves) different? How are the petals (leaves) the same?

Explore

Read the task aloud and hand out a set of small flower cutouts (see following page) to each pair of students. Ask students to work with their partner to sort the flowers into the two baskets so that the flowers in each basket are similar in some way.

Ask the following questions to check for understanding:

- How did you sort your flowers?
- How did you know which flowers to place in each basket?
- How do you know there are _____ petals (leaves) on this flower? Can you show me how you counted?
- Which basket has the most (fewest) flowers? How do you know?

Next, give each student pair two different colored sheets of construction paper to represent the two baskets. Have students glue their flowers onto the appropriate "basket."

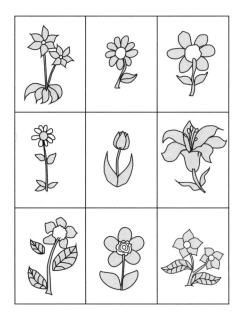

Summarize

Start by asking, "Who has just one flower in a basket? How many are in your other basket?" Have these students share how they chose to sort the flowers. If they sorted by the number of petals or leaves, ask students to explain their counting strategy to the class. If they sorted by another attribute, such as the shape of the petals or leaves, ask them to describe and point out these attributes on each flower. Continue this process until all the student pairs have shared their work.

Differentiation

- To support struggling students, decrease the number of flowers.
- To support struggling students, provide the categories the students should use to sort the flowers.
- To support struggling students, include only flowers that can be easily sorted into two distinct groups, for example, two leaves and three leaves, five petals and six petals, and small flowers and big flowers.
- To support students who struggle to keep track of which petals they counted, provide manipulatives they can use to cover the petals as they count them.
- To extend this task, ask students to sort the flowers into more than two categories.
- To extend this task, take students on a walk and have them draw pictures of the flowers they see.

SAND CASTLES

Mazie and her family went to the beach for summer vacation. When a large wave crashed into the shore, her sand castle was washed away. The next day, Mazie decided to build a new sand castle. Use the footprints of Mazie's sand toys to help her create a new sand castle.

CCSSM STANDARD FOR MATHEMATICAL PRACTICE

Practice 6: Attend to precision.

CCSSM STANDARD FOR MATHEMATICAL CONTENT

K.G.B.4: Analyze and compare two- and three-dimensional shapes, in different sizes and orientations, using informal language to describe their similarities, differences, parts (e.g., number of sides and vertices/"corners") and other attributes (e.g., having sides of equal length).

PROBLEM DISCUSSION

This task provides a context for students within which to explore three-dimensional shapes by having them construct sand castles using a variety of classroom objects such as pattern blocks, logic blocks, three-dimensional geometric figures, and other manipulatives. This semistructured block-building task helps students develop spatial skills, preparing them for CCSSM kindergarten standards related to analyzing, comparing, creating, and composing shapes (K.G.B.4, K.G.B.5, K.G.B.6). Specifically, students use two-dimensional shapes as footprints for selecting three-dimensional shapes to create the foundation of a sand castle. They then stack other three-dimensional shapes onto the foundation to create the castle.

Students build their castles using a variety of three-dimensional shapes. The task encourages math talk among students as they describe their sand castles, including the similarities and differences between two- and three-dimensional shapes. These discussions help lead students from a visual level to a descriptive level of geometric thinking (Moomaw 2011). According to the van Hiele Levels of Geometric Thinking, students at the descriptive level of thinking describe shapes based on their attributes (van Hiele 1999). For example, students may describe shapes on the basis of the number of faces or "sides," whether or not the shape can roll, which two-dimensional figures are visible in the three-dimensional shape, whether or not the shape has a "point" (vertex), and so on. Model correct academic language and encourage students to focus on clear descriptions of the blocks that make up their sand castle (SMP 6). They may "initially use their own terms and language and increasingly adopt mathematical language" (Fuson, Clements, and Beckmann 2010, p. 52), such as transitioning from *ball* to *sphere* or from *can* to *cylinder*.

STRATEGIES

- Students may experiment with a variety of shapes.
- Students may find a shape that matches a footprint and use only this shape as the foundation.
- Students may find more than one shape that matches a footprint and use these shapes as parts of the foundation.
- Students may create a sand castle that is symmetrical.

MISCONCEPTIONS/STUDENT DIFFICULTIES

- Students may not realize they can arrange multiple shapes to build layers onto their sand castle.
- Students may have difficulty stacking shapes so the sand castle does not topple.
- Students may not realize there can be gaps and overlaps between shapes.
- Students may use informal academic language, such as calling a rectangular prism a "rectangle" or a "box" or referring to the faces as "sides."

LAUNCH

Give students a variety of three-dimensional shapes (e.g., pattern blocks, logic blocks, three-dimensional geometric figures, and other manipulatives). Begin by asking students to work with a partner to sort the shapes into two categories. Categories could include "will roll," "all faces are rectangles," "one or more faces are a triangle," "has a point or vertex," and so on. Once students have sorted the shapes into two categories, ask partners to describe their categories to the class.

Ask these questions to check for understanding:

- Are these shapes two-dimensional or three-dimensional? How do you know?
- How do you know this shape fits your category?
- Point to different faces of a shape and ask which two-dimensional shapes they see.
- Point to two shapes and ask how the two shapes are similar or different.

If students do not come up with the categories described above, prompt them to sort on the basis of these groups. When students use informal language, point out the more academic language that will be used in kindergarten; for example, "sides" of a three- dimensional shape are referred to as *faces*, "balls" as *spheres*, "boxes" as *prisms*, and "cans" as *cylinders*.

Ask students if they have ever built or seen a sand castle. Have them describe the sand castle to their partner. If students have not had an experience with sand castles, display a picture of one. Tell students that today they will be helping Mazie create her sand castle, but first they must look at the "footprints" of all of the sand toys Mazie used to build her castle.

Show students the footprints. (These footprints are just examples of possible shapes and may not be the exact size of the bases of the three-dimensional shapes you have available in your classroom.) Ask students to find a shape they recognize and share with the class what they notice about the shape. Do this for each of the footprint shapes. Next, explain to students that they will help Mazie create a new sand castle.

EXPLORE

Have students work with a partner to complete the task.

Ask the following questions to check for understanding:

- Are these footprints two-dimensional or three-dimensional shapes? How do you know?
- How many sides does this footprint have?
- Point to two shapes and ask how the shapes are similar and how they are different.

Ask students to work with a partner to find at least one three-dimensional shape that has a similar footprint to the ones Mazie used to make her sand castle. Read the task to students. Have students individually create a sand castle using three-dimensional shapes.

Ask questions like the following to check for understanding:

- Can you use more than ____ blocks to build the sand castle?
- Could Mazie use more than one shape for the bottom of her sand castle?
- Could Mazie build a sand castle that has a window or a door?
- Which shapes did you use in your sand castle?

SUMMARIZE

Ask students to describe their sand castle to their partner, characterizing each shape and its location (they may use informal and formal terms [can/cylinder, box/prism/cube, point/vertex, ball/sphere, etc.]). Model the description by using sentences such as the following:

- The bottom of my sand castle is a _____.
- On top of the _____ is a _____. (Repeat as necessary.)
- The top of my sand castle is a _____.

To conclude the task, ask students to share which shapes worked best as foundation shapes for building the sand castle and why. The cones, pyramids, and spheres may be shared as ones that do not work well as foundation shapes because they do not allow for other shapes to be stacked upon them.

DIFFERENTIATION

- To support struggling students, limit the shapes to only those that stack, by excluding the pyramids, cones, and spheres.
- To support struggling students, limit the number of footprints.
- To support struggling students, start their sand castle for them. For example, use two prisms as the foundation and allow the student to continue building from that point.
- To extend the task, ask students to create a sand castle using specific shapes. For example, ask, "Can you create a sand castle that has three prisms (boxes) and two pyramids?" or "Can you make a sand castle that uses six shapes?"
- To extend this task, take a picture of each sand castle and record students' descriptions of their sand castles.

SIDEWALK CHALK SHAPES

One morning Mr. Allen's students drew 10 different shapes on the sidewalk using chalk. Before they could share their shapes, a rain shower washed away some of the chalk. Mr. Allen took a picture of the ruined shapes. Using the pictures, can you help the students remember what their shapes looked like before the rain?

CCSSM STANDARD FOR MATHEMATICAL PRACTICE

Practice 3: Construct viable arguments and critique the reasoning of others.

CCSSM STANDARDS FOR MATHEMATICAL CONTENT

K.G.A.2: Correctly name shapes regardless of their orientations or overall size.

K.G.B.4: Analyze and compare two- and three-dimensional shapes, in different sizes and orientations, using informal language to describe their similarities, differences, parts (e.g., number of sides and vertices/"corners") and other attributes (e.g., having sides of equal length).

PROBLEM DISCUSSION

In prekindergarten, children are exposed to many shapes and begin to talk about those they see around them. Specifically, students in early grades "should create mental images of geometric shapes using spatial memory and spatial visualization" as well as "recognize and represent shapes from different perspectives" (NCTM 2000, p. 96). As students reconstruct the partial shapes on the handout, they are able to develop their spatial reasoning skills by generating a mental image of each shape and maintaining this mental image in order to complete the shape, which may require them to rotate or resize the mental image (Clements and Sarama 2009).

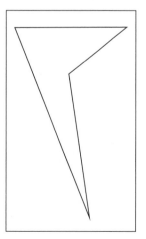

As this task is open-ended (e.g., a student can see a right angle and construct a right triangle, square, rectangle, or another shape), students are able to draw upon their knowledge of two-dimensional shapes when they identify, create, describe, and compare shapes with a partner (K.G.A.2 and K.G.B.4). Students are encouraged to draw ten different shapes. This may be difficult for some students because they may have a narrow view of shape classes. For example, if they create a triangle out of the right angles, they may see these as two different shapes because the shapes are rotated. In addition, the partial shapes were selected to encourage the creation of a variety of shapes, which may include convex as well as concave ones. If students draw a concave shape like the one to the right, a discussion about the number of vertices, or corners, may ensue.

Through discussions, students are able to practice informal and formal language to identify defining attributes of their shapes. In addition, by comparing and contrasting their shapes with those of others, students will need to critique the reasoning of their peers (SMP 3). Whether they are operating at the visual level or the descriptive level of the van Hiele Geometric Levels of Thinking, this task offers students the chance to grapple with their schema for shape (van Hiele 1999) and provides "experiences that support visual concepts and help children transition from the visual to the descriptive level" (Moomaw 2011, p. 99). For example, when describing a shape, a student at the visual level may say, "It's a triangle because it looks like a triangle," whereas a student at the descriptive level may say, "It's a triangle because it has three sides."

STRATEGIES

- Students may simply connect the two end points using a straight or a curved line.
- Students may try to recreate the other "half" of the shape based on their ideas of symmetry.
- Students may draw a complete shape on another piece of paper and then try to find a partial shape that could be used to make that shape.
- Students may draw common shapes (circles, triangles, rectangles, hexagons, etc.).
- Students may draw shapes that are concave.

MISCONCEPTIONS/STUDENT DIFFICULTIES

- Students may have a limited vocabulary for describing their shapes.
- Students may have difficulty recognizing common shapes that have been rotated. For example, if students create a triangle out of the acute angle, they do not recognize it as a triangle because it does not have a vertex "pointing up."
- Students may create the same shape, but do not recognize it as the same, only rotated.
- Students may be unable to think of shapes beyond the common ones and cannot create ten different shapes.

LAUNCH

To begin, draw a familiar shape on the board; then cover a portion of the shape. Ask students to talk to a partner about what the shape might look like. Encourage them to draw the shape. Ask the following questions to encourage students to share some of their ideas in order to focus on the descriptive words they use, recording them for students to reference later:

- Did anyone draw a shape with three (four or five) straight sides?
- Do we have a name for this shape?
- How many vertices (corners) does your shape have?
- Did anyone draw a shape with curved lines?
- Did anyone draw a shape that was not closed?

Next, ask students to create their own shape on paper. Explain to them that they will use a second piece of paper to hide part of their shape. Ask students to show their work to a partner. The partner's job is to draw what he thinks the complete shape is. Next, have students reveal their shapes, and compare and contrast the actual shape to the predicted shape. Encourage students to focus on descriptive words like those previously discussed. After they have described their shapes to a partner, have students share the descriptive words with the class. Keep track of the words for students to see. This list may include curved lines, straight sides, corners, vertices, number of sides, number of corners or vertices, closed, shape names, slanty, pointy, skinny, and so on.

Explore

Read the task aloud to students. Give each student the chalk shapes handout. Remind students that the ten shapes should be different shapes. As students complete this task, encourage them to describe their shapes to their peers. Because this task may help students transition from the visual to the descriptive level, they may need prompting to attend to the defining characteristics of each shape they draw. Students who struggle to think of a variety of shapes can be encouraged to "spy" on others to gather ideas for different types of shapes.

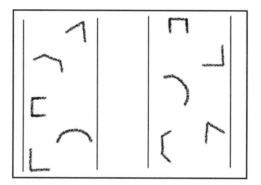

Questions to ask students who are operating at a *visual level* (e.g., "This is a square because it looks like a square.") may include the following:

- What do you notice about the shape?
- How many sides does it have?
- Are the lines straight or curvy?
- What do you notice about the length of the sides?
- How many vertices (corners) does the shape have?

Questions to ask students who are operating at or transitioning to a *descriptive level* (e.g., "This is a square because it has four sides.") may include the following:

- (*Pointing to two of their shapes*) What is the same about the shapes? What is different about the shapes?
- What is always true about triangles (rectangles, squares, etc.)? Can you draw another triangle that is different from the ones you have already drawn?

- If students struggle to recognize a shape that has been rotated from the typical orientation, rotate the student's paper until the shape is in the common position. Ask the student what the shape is called. For example, if a student does not recognize a triangle that has been rotated, rotate the shape so one side is parallel to the floor and ask, "Is this a triangle?" Then continue to rotate the shape slightly, and each time ask, "Is it still a triangle?"

SUMMARIZE

Ask students to choose two of their favorite shapes to share with a partner, and have them take turns describing their shapes to each other. Remind students to use informal as well as formal descriptive words like those created in the list from the Launch. As students describe their shapes to their partners, encourage them to use words that do not appear on the list from the Launch. Next, ask students to share any descriptive words they used that were not on the original list. Add these words to the list for students to see the many different attributes a shape can have. These descriptive words should be the focus of the summary.

To conclude this task, ask students questions such as the following, and have them take turns sharing their shapes and explaining why each shape meets the criteria:

- Did anyone draw a shape with three (four or five) straight sides? How do you know?
- Do we have a name for this shape?
- How many vertices, or corners, does your shape have? How do you know?
- Did anyone draw a shape with curved lines? How do you know?
- Did anyone draw a shape that was not closed? How do you know?

DIFFERENTIATION

- To support struggling students, provide pictures of familiar shapes.
- To support struggling students, have students create shapes on half the sidewalk (five shapes in total).
- To support struggling students, enlarge the handout so students have more room to draw their shapes.
- To extend the task, give students a premade set of ten shapes and ask them to determine if all ten shapes are different.
- To challenge students, give them clues to a completed shape. After listening to the clues, have them either point to the shape or actually create the shape from a portion of the shape. For example, show them a right angle and say, "My shape has two straight sides, one curved line, and one vertex. What does my shape look like?"

A WEEKEND CAMPING TRIP

Twelve people are going on a camping trip. They are taking the following types of tents:

- 6 two-person tents
- 4 three-person tents
- 2 six-person tents

Show how you could arrange the 12 campers in tents so everyone has a place to sleep. Make a drawing or write an equation to show your thinking.

CCSSM Standards for Mathematical Practice

Practice 2: Reason abstractly and quantitatively.

Practice 4: Model with mathematics.

CCSSM Standards for Mathematical Content

K.CC.A.3: Write numbers from 0 to 20. Represent a number of objects with a written numeral 0–20 (with 0 representing a count of no objects).

K.OA.A.1: Represent addition and subtraction with objects, fingers, mental images, drawings, sounds (e.g., claps), acting out situations, verbal explanations, expressions, or equations.

Problem Discussion

This problem asks kindergarten students to identify ways to arrange and account for twelve items. Students are asked to write numbers (K.CC.A.3) as well as represent addition of addends in multiple ways (K.OA.A.1). The twelve items are campers, who must be arranged in tents for a weekend camping trip. Tents hold up to two, three, or six people each.

The tents that are available hold up to thirty-six people when filled to capacity, so there are multiple ways to arrange the campers using as few as two tents or as many as all twelve tents. Students may choose to use only one type of tent and fill these to capacity (first three rows of the table below). Or, they may explore other possibilities if tents are not filled to capacity. Possible combinations are represented in rows of the table on the following page.

Two-Person Tents						Three-Person Tents				Six-Person Tents	
2	2	2	2	2	2						
						3	3	3	3		
										6	6
2	2	2				3	3				
1	1	1	1	1	1					6	
2	2	1				2	2			3	

Throughout this task, children are asked to reason abstractly about the problem's context, first representing people with manipulatives and ultimately as numerals, while also portraying tents as addends (SMP 2). For example, to represent the first row of the table with an equation, each addend represents a quantity of people as well as depicting a tent $(2 + 2 + 2 + 2 + 2 + 2 = 12)$. Although writing an equation is not a requirement of this task, this process provides kindergarten students an additional opportunity to model with mathematics (SMP 4).

STRATEGIES

- Students may use manipulatives to represent the twelve campers and distribute them in the available tents.
- Students may place campers in tents, recounting the number of campers each time a new camper is put in a tent.
- Students may arrange campers in tents to each tent's capacity before using another tent.
- Students may distribute campers to tents, one per tent, until a tent is full or the campers are all distributed.
- Students may draw campers (e.g., stick figures, dots) to represent people in each tent.
- Students may attribute numerals for the number of campers in each tent, and then add these values to check if twelve campers have been accounted for.

MISCONCEPTIONS/STUDENT DIFFICULTIES

- Students may incorrectly assume they need to use either all the tents or as few tents as possible.
- Students may have difficulty understanding that the size of the tent indicates the person capacity of the tent.
- Students may confuse the person capacity of the tent with the number of people that they have assigned to the tent.
- Students may have difficulty counting twelve objects when they are not arranged in a line or circle.
- Students may have difficulty adding multiple addends together.

LAUNCH

Find out how many students have been camping before. Ask these children where they slept when they were camping—a tent, a camper, and so forth. If any students have camped in tents, ask them who else slept in their tents and how many people the tent could hold.

Tell students about different size tents, and how they are typically classified by the number of people that can sleep comfortably in the tent. If possible, show the students pictures of different tents, perhaps from a website of an outdoor recreation store.

Sketch a small two-person tent and a larger six-person tent. Label these tents based on how many people the tents can hold, and ask, "How many people would be able to sleep in these two tents?" After students have explained their thinking, add a sketch of a three-person tent. "How many people would be able to sleep in these three tents?" Have students share their thinking. Some may count again from the beginning; others may add three to the previous sum. Write an equation on the board to represent the total number of people for these three tents: $2 + 6 + 3 = 11$.

Read the task aloud to students. Make sure that students understand the context, and that twelve people will be camping. Ask students to predict whether or not the tents that are available will be enough to hold all twelve people and to share their reasoning about their predictions.

EXPLORE

Provide a small bag of the tent pictures to pairs of students. Ask each pair to find at least one way to arrange the twelve campers in the tents. Also provide twenty Unifix cubes to each team so they can model the people in the tents. More than enough Unifix cubes are provided so students are required to count out the twelve and confirm that they have accounted for twelve campers—not more or fewer.

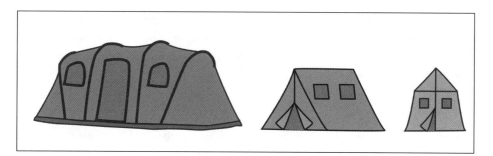

As students work on the problem, ask the following questions to check for understanding:

- Which tents have you decided to use? How many people do you have sleeping in each of your tents?
- Do all twelve people have a tent to sleep in? How do you know?
- Do you think there is another way you could arrange the twelve people in the tents?

- Can you write an equation that shows how you have arranged people in the tents?
- Can you explain to me where this 3 (or other quantity) in your equation comes from?

Students do not have to generate more than one answer to the problem, but use this opportunity to assess whether the students understand the concept of exchanging—in this case, people moving from one tent to another, decreasing the quantity in one tent but increasing the quantity in the other.

Also, attend to students' abilities to determine the sum of the people who have been accounted for in the tents. This is a good opportunity to assess which students are counting all, and which ones might be using other strategies for combining single-digit quantities.

Finally, ask each pair to make a poster of their sleeping arrangements for the camping trip. Tents can be pasted on the posters, along with some indication of the number of people in each tent (e.g., pictures, dots, stickers). Challenge students to include an equation representing their sleeping solution.

SUMMARIZE

Hang students' posters throughout the room, and have students do a gallery walk to see their classmates' ways of arranging twelve people in tents. As students examine the work of their classmates, ask some of them to confirm that twelve people have been accounted for in the tents. This is a good opportunity to assess students' counting or addition skills.

When students have finished their gallery walk, ask, "Did anyone find the way of putting twelve people in tents that used the fewest number of tents?" The fewest number of tents that can be used is two: $6 + 6 = 12$. Write down the equation and ask the class how they know how many tents were used (the number of addends). Ask, "What kinds of tents were used? How do you know?"

Similarly, ask the class if they can identify an arrangement that used the most number of tents. Write this equation and ask, "How do you know how many tents were used? What kinds of tents were they? How do you know?" Also, this arrangement can be tied back to students' own camping experiences: "Why might it be nice to have fewer people in each tent?" Students who have camped before may comment that it is more comfortable to have some extra room in a tent.

Finally, choose two or three representations from other posters and discuss and transform them into an equation (if not already provided). Ask students how they can prove that this arrangement accounts for all twelve people on the camping trip. For each situation, ask several students to share their strategies for counting the number of people in tents. Some students will count all. Others may use other strategies (e.g., making ten) to combine quantities.

If possible, ask students to compare equations. For example, they might compare $6 + 6 = 12$ and $6 + 3 + 3 = 12$. They may notice that one of the addends in the equations is the same. In the second equation, one of the sixes from the first equation has been replaced by 2 threes. Ask, "Is there a way that you could know that this second equation adds up to twelve by comparing it to what we know about the first equation?"

If there is time, explore finding different ways to arrange twelve campers using all of the available tents.

DIFFERENTIATION

- For struggling students, limit the number of campers to eight or ten.
- For struggling students, reduce the number of types of tents available. For example, only provide two-person tents and three-person tents.
- For students who have quickly found one way to arrange the twelve campers, ask them to do it again using either as few tents as possible or all the tents.
- Ask students how many people could be accommodated if all the tents were filled to capacity.
- Ask students to determine how they might arrange the twelve campers if eight were adults and four were children.
- For students who need an additional challenge, ask them to determine how they might arrange twenty campers in the available tents.

July 4th Celebration

To celebrate Independence Day, Kelsey and Carter went to different parades with their families. Kelsey's parade started and ended at the times below.

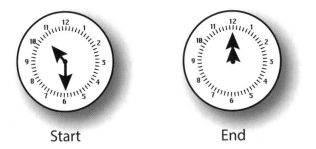

Start   End

Carter's parade started at 11:00 a.m. He forgot to look at his watch when the parade ended. If Carter's parade was longer than Kelsey's, what time could his parade have ended?

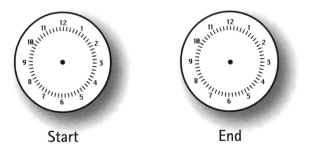

Start   End

CCSSM Standard for Mathematical Practice

Practice 5: Use appropriate tools strategically.

CCSSM Standard for Mathematical Content

1.MD.B.3: Tell and write time in hours and half-hours using analog and digital clocks.

Problem Discussion

According to the National Council of Teachers of Mathematics (2000), students should be provided opportunities to "focus on time and its measurement through short conversations. … As teachers call attention to the clock, many young students will learn to tell time" (p. 104). This task allows students to model time as well as the duration of a time interval through the use of different tools, such as an analog clock, a digital clock, and a time line (SMP 5). Students will need to read times on an analog clock to the hour and half hour (1.MD.B.3).

In this early stage of learning to tell time, there are many aspects that students must understand. For example, they must be able to place and know the distinction between the hour and minute hands on an analog clock as well as know the direction in which the hands are moving. Students must also "understand that each number on the clock has two different meanings, relate the positions of the hands to the meaning of the numbers, and finally, tell the time" (Fiederwitzer and Berman 1999, p. 255).

This task also allows students to explore the notion of elapsed time in an authentic context, leading to 3.MD.A.1, in which students determine elapsed time. As students describe elapsed time, they will further develop the concept of units of time, especially the units of one hour and a half hour. When finding elapsed time, students may use ideas of regrouping or decomposing (e.g., sixty minutes is two groups of thirty minutes or two half-hour intervals) from their previous work with whole numbers (K.NBT.A.1). An early strategy for finding elapsed time includes the use of a number line. Students are introduced to the number line when working with whole numbers (1.NBT.C4). This model can be extended in the form of a time line, which helps students visualize and represent intervals of time.

10:00   10:30   11:00   11:30   12:00   12:30   1:00   1:30

STRATEGIES

- Students may use skip counting to determine the time on each analog clock.
- Students may know from memory that the number 6 on the analog clock can represent both the hour six and thirty minutes, depending on which hand is associated with the 6.
- Students may skip-count by half-hour intervals to find there are three half-hour intervals between 10:30 and 12:00.
- Students may count on first by one hour to reach 11:30, and then add one more half hour to find the interval of one and one-half hours.

MISCONCEPTIONS/STUDENT DIFFICULTIES

- Students may struggle to understand a.m. versus p.m.
- Students may struggle to remember that on an analog clock the long hand is associated with minutes and the short hand with hours.
- Students may not understand that each number of the analog clock can represent both the hour of the day as well as the number of minutes.
- Students may count the three thirty-minute intervals, but record them as three hours instead of one hour thirty minutes.

Launch

Ask students if they and their families have ever gone to see a parade. Ask which holiday they were celebrating when they did this. Next, ask students at what time of day they usually watch parades. After a reasonable time is offered, record itthat time on the board, and discuss whether this is in the morning or evening and how this can be shown on a digital clock. Ask students to share other things they do to celebrate the holidays they have mentioned. Have students pick one event and record the time on a digital clock using a.m. or p.m.

Ask the following questions to check for understanding:

- What time do you usually eat breakfast? Lunch? Dinner?
- Does your event happen before or after breakfast? Lunch? Dinner?

Once they have made a record of their clocks, have students discuss their events, times, and clocks with a partner. After partners agree that the event and time are reasonable, ask students to share their events and clocks with the class. As students report, model how to record the digital time on an analog clock, allowing students to follow along on their own analog clock manipulatives or blank paper clocks.

Ask the following questions to check for understanding:

- Which hand tells us the hour? Which hand tells us the minutes?
- How many minutes does each number on the clock represent?
- Will you skip-count by fives to show me which number represents thirty minutes?
- How do you know the twelve represents zero minutes or o'clock?
- What's another way to say eight thirty? (You want an answer like "half past eight" or "halfway between eight o'clock and nine o'clock.")
- How are the analog and digital clocks the same and how are they different? (For example, analog clocks do not identify a.m. or p.m., digital clocks do not rely on knowing how many minutes are represented by each digit. Both types of clocks represent the number of hours and minutes past the hour.)

Explore

Hand out the task to students and read the task aloud. Ask students to work individually or with a partner to determine the digital time for each of Kelsey's clocks.

Ask questions like the following to check for understanding:

- Which hand tells us the hour? Which hand tells us the minutes?
- How many minutes does each number on the clock represent?
- Will you skip-count by fives to show me which number represents thirty minutes?
- How do you know the twelve represents o'clock?
- Is this time an a.m. time or a p.m. time?

Once students have agreed that Kelsey's parade began at 10:30 a.m. and ended at 12:00 p.m., students should then determine the duration of her parade. Students may be encouraged to use a time line to help model the interval of time. Strategies using the time line may include intervals of thirty minutes or one interval of an hour and one interval of thirty minutes.

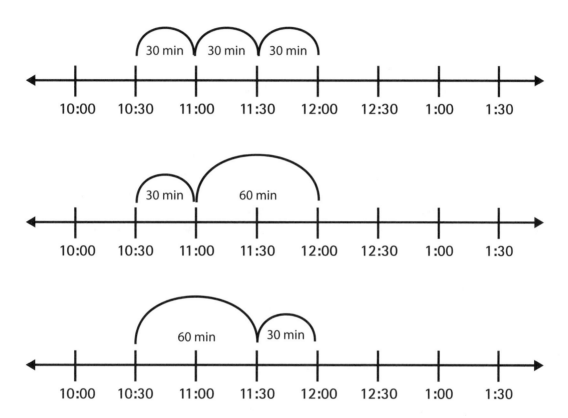

Next, reread the second part of the task. Ask students to create an analog clock to display the beginning time of Carter's parade. Encourage students to record this time on a new time line. Ask students to work with their partner to determine what could be a possible ending for Carter's parade. As students work, take note of the different strategies they use to determine elapsed time.

SUMMARIZE

Ask partners to work with another pair to check their answer for the length of Kelsey's parade. Then have students share their solution strategies with the whole class. If the three time-line strategies shown above are not mentioned, show them and ask students to determine if they are correct representations of the duration of the parade. Note that some students may say the length was "ninety minutes" while others may give some permutation of "one and one-half hours." Discuss how these two times are the same using the models students provide.

Next, ask students to record the times they chose for Carter's parade to end. Ask, "Which of these times makes the shortest (or longest) parade for Carter?" Note that there are a variety of possible answers. For example, if students choose not to create a time that is at the hour or half hour, make sure they are able to explain how they produced their clock. Ask those students who shared the shortest and longest times to draw and explain the analog clocks they created for these times.

Ask the following questions to check for understanding:

- How did you create your analog clock?
- How did you know where to put the long hand and the short hand?
- Is your time an a.m. time or a p.m. time?

Ask partners to work with another pair to check their clocks for Carter's beginning and ending parade times. Circulate around the room to ensure students are creating their analog clocks correctly. Next, ask students to share strategies for how they determined the length of Carter's parade. Again, if the strategies like those above are not used, encourage students to use the time line to model their thinking. To conclude, ask students to talk with their partners to determine how much longer Carter's parade was than Kelsey's parade. Students can then work with another group to share their strategies.

DIFFERENTIATION

- To support struggling students, put the number of minutes above each number on the clock to aid in skip counting.
- To support struggling students, have the parades begin at the same time.
- To support struggling students, provide a time line like the one shown in the Problem Discussion.
- To extend this task, have students measure elapsed time using times to the nearest quarter hour.
- To extend this task, ask students, "What time would Kelsey's parade need to start to be the same length as Carter's parade?"

Baseball Ticket Sales

The Lancer Baseball Stadium needs repairs, and the seats will be replaced one section at a time, starting with the section that has the most ticket sales. The number of tickets sold for the four sections are 39, 40, 50, and 53. Use the clues below to help the team figure out how many tickets are sold in each section of the stadium.

Clue 1: The fewest number of tickets was sold in Section D.

Clue 2: The number of tickets sold in Section C has a zero in the ones place.

Clue 3: There were more tickets sold in Section A than in Section C.

Clue 4: The difference between the combined ticket sales in Sections A and B and Sections C and D is 4 tickets.

CCSSM Standard for Mathematical Practice

Practice 5: Use appropriate tools strategically.

CCSSM Standards for Mathematical Content

1.NBT.B.3: Compare two two-digit numbers based on meanings of the tens and ones digits, recording the results of comparisons with the symbols >, =, and <.

1.NBT.C.4: Add within 100, including adding a two-digit number and a one-digit number, and adding a two-digit number and a multiple of 10, using concrete models or drawings and strategies based on place value, properties of operations, and/or the relationship between addition and subtraction; relate the strategy to a written method and explain the reasoning used. Understand that in adding two-digit numbers, one adds tens and tens, ones and ones; and sometimes it is necessary to compose a ten.

Problem Discussion

In this task students will apply place-value concepts to compare, add, and subtract two-digit numbers (1.NBT.B.3; 1.NBT.C.4). In first grade, students continue to develop understanding of addition and subtraction by exploring different strategies and models, including discrete objects, length models, and number lines (Caldwell, Karp, and Bay-Williams 2011). Clue 4 requires students to add and subtract a two-digit number with a multiple of ten for which they can use a variety of strategies, such as concrete manipulatives, drawings, and place value. Students must also understand academic language such as *more, fewest,* and *difference.* For example, clues 1, 3, and 4 require students to understand how to compare 2 two-digit numbers to determine which section had more or fewer tickets sold. This task offers a context that encourages students to use a variety of representations to show, compare, and add two-digit numbers (SMP 5).

Due to the lengthy clues, this task will likely need to be facilitated by the teacher. The Explore section offers a way for students to engage in the problem-solving process once

each clue has been read to them. Although this task has one correct solution, students use problem-solving strategies to explore different number combinations to satisfy each of the four clues. As students work through the clues, they begin to eliminate choices. Clue 1 allows students to find the number of tickets sold in Section D using place-value concepts to compare two-digit numbers. Clue 2 requires students to understand that a zero in the ones place means that after grouping ones into tens, there are no ones left over. This clue, however, only eliminates one of the remaining choices, leaving two choices for the number of tickets sold in Section C. Students then need to work through clues 3 and 4 using a variety of addition, subtraction, and comparison strategies to determine that the number of tickets sold in Section A is 53, Section B is 40, Section C is 50, and Section D is 39.

STRATEGIES

- Students may use a guess-and-check process to determine if their answer meets each criterion.
- After each clue is read, students may narrow down the possibilities until they have only those that will satisfy each clue.
- Students may use manipulatives or drawings to represent each number of tickets and use a matching strategy to compare numbers.
- Students may use place-value concepts to compare the numbers. For example, 39 is less than 50 because 39 has only 3 tens.
- Students may directly model the quantities in the problem (e.g., base-ten blocks), and use the model to combine numbers by counting all or counting on by ones.
- Students may break the quantities apart by place value and use partial sums to find the combined total number of tickets.
- Students may use an open number line or another tool to add together the ticket quantities for sections A and B and sections C and D, and then compare the two sums.
- Students may count on by skip-counting by tens to find the sum.

MISCONCEPTIONS/STUDENT DIFFICULTIES

- Students may misinterpret or not understand the meaning of the words *more*, *fewest*, and *difference*.
- Students may not realize there can be more than one possibility after clue 2 has been read.
- Students may struggle to organize their thinking because there is more than one solution that satisfies clues 2, 3, and 4.
- Students may make common addition or subtraction errors, either with facts or with algorithms.

LAUNCH

Ask, "How many baseballs do you think are used in a major league baseball game?" Pick two major league teams that students are familiar with, such as the Chicago Cubs and the New York Yankees. Pose the scenario that in the Chicago Cubs' game, fifty baseballs were used and in the New York Yankees' game, forty-six baseballs were used. Ask students to determine at which game fewer baseballs were used.

Ask the following questions to check for understanding:

- Can you use manipulatives or drawings to represent each number?
- How many groups of ten can you make for each number? How do you know?
- How many ones are left over for each number? How do you know?

Ask students to share their explanations for which team used more baseballs. Prompt students to state the answer in multiple ways in order to reinforce terms such as *fewer/less* and *greater/more*. For example, "The Yankees used fewer baseballs than the Cubs. The Cubs used more baseballs than the Yankees."

Next, ask students to work with a partner to find the combined total number of baseballs the two teams used. Encourage students to find more than one way to find this total.

Ask these questions to check for understanding:

- What number do you think the total is close to? Why?
- How can you use manipulatives or drawings to represent each number?
- Can you skip-count by tens to help you count on to find the total?

Have students share their solution strategies, beginning with students who used concrete models or drawings, followed by students who used place-value strategies.

EXPLORE

Ask students if they have ever attended a baseball game. Engage in a discussion about stadiums and how large stadiums are divided into sections. A picture of a stadium may be helpful in visualizing the context of the task. Explain to students that the Lancer Stadium needs repairs, and the team wants to know how many tickets are sold in each section of the stadium so it can plan which section is to be remodeled first. Tell them that "The supervisor of ticket sales knows that usually there are 53, 39, 40, and 50 tickets sold in the four sections, but does not remember which number of tickets goes with which section of the stadium. She does remember some information about the ticket sales." Hand out and read the task to students. Write the four ticket-sales numbers on the board as well as the table from the handout. Read the first clue to the class. Ask students to discuss with a partner what this clue tells them about the number of tickets in Section D.

As students work with their partner to determine the smallest number, ask the following questions to check for understanding:

- What does the word *fewest* mean?
- Can you use manipulatives or drawings to represent each number?
- How many groups of ten does each number have?

Have students share their thoughts with the class. Once everyone has agreed that there were 39 tickets sold in Section D, record this in the table and cross out the 39 from the list of ticket sales.

Next, read clue 2. Ask students to talk with their partners about what this clue tells them about the number of tickets sold in Section C.

Section A	Section B	Section C	Section D
			39
Sections A and B combined		Sections C and D combined	

As students work with their partners to determine the number of tickets sold in Section C, ask these questions to check for understanding:

- Could the number of tickets sold in Section C be 53? Explain.
- If a number has a zero in the ones place, what would that look like using your drawing or manipulatives?
- Is there another number that has no ones?

Have students share their thoughts with the class. Once everyone has agreed that Section C has either 40 or 50 tickets sold, record those possibilities in the table. At this point, it may be helpful to create a second table so that the 40 and 50 do not appear in the same box.

Section A	Section B	Section C	Section D
		50	39
Sections A and B combined		Sections C and D combined	

Section A	Section B	Section C	Section D
		40	39
Sections A and B combined		Sections C and D combined	

Next, read clue 3. Ask students to talk with their partners about what this clue tells them about the number of tickets sold in Sections A and C.

As students work with their partner to determine the possibilities for the number of tickets sold in Sections A and C ask the following questions to check for understanding:

- What number of tickets is the largest number? How do you know?
- Could the number of tickets sold in Section A be 40? How do you know?

Have students share their thoughts with the class. As students talk, record the possibilities on the board using the tables. If students do not share all of the possibilities, use the questions below to help elicit all possibilities:

- If Section C has 50 tickets sold, how many tickets would Section A have sold?
- If Section C has 40 tickets sold, how many tickets would Section A have sold? Is that the only possibility for Section A?

Section A	Section B	Section C	Section D
53		50	39
Sections A and B combined		Sections C and D combined	

Section A	Section B	Section C	Section D
50		40	39
Sections A and B combined		Sections C and D combined	

Section A	Section B	Section C	Section D
53		40	39
Sections A and B combined		Sections C and D combined	

Read clue 4. Ask students to talk with their partner about what this clue tells them about the number of tickets sold in Sections A and B and Sections C and D. Have students work with their partner to form a plan for finding the combined totals. As students begin working to find the combinations for each of the three situations shown in the tables above, note that the combination of 50 and 53 will be more than 100.

As students work to combine section totals, ask these questions to check for understanding:

- How can you use manipulatives or drawings to represent each number?
- Can you use skip counting by tens to help you count on to find the total?
- What number do you get when you have ten groups of 10?

SUMMARIZE

Have students share their results, and record them in tables like the ones below. Ask students to explain how they combined the total ticket sales for Sections A and B and Sections C and D. Encourage students who combined the ticket sales in a different way to share their strategies. If students do not present each of the three possibilities below, refer back to the tables that were created after reading clue 3 to elicit any of the missing possibilities. Next, have students verify why only one of the three possibilities is a viable answer. Again, have students share their strategies for determining whether there is a difference of four seats.

To conclude this activity, ask students to reflect upon the problem-solving process with their partner. Have them reread the clues and ask students to think about which clue they found easiest to work with and why. Then have students share their thoughts with the class. Next, ask students to think about which clue they found most challenging and why. Again, have students share their thoughts with the class. Finally, ask students to place the sections in order from greatest to least. Then have them talk to their partner about which section they would suggest the Lancer Baseball Team remodel first and why.

Section A	Section B	Section C	Section D
53	40	50	39
Sections A and B combined		Sections C and D combined	
93		89	

Section A	Section B	Section C	Section D
50	53	40	39
Sections A and B combined		Sections C and D combined	
103		79	

Section A	Section B	Section C	Section D
53	50	40	39
Sections A and B combined		Sections C and D combined	
103		79	

DIFFERENTIATION

- To support struggling students, provide handouts with all the tables.
- To support struggling students, make the numbers smaller by taking away the same amount from each number (e.g., 33, 30, 20, and 19).
- To extend the task, ask students to create a new clue 4 so that one a different solution satisfies the four clues.
- To extend this task, make the numbers larger by adding the same amount to each number (e.g., 83, 80, 70, and 69).
- To extend the task, ask students to write a letter to the Lancer Baseball Team suggesting the order in which sections should be repaired.

Swimming at Swan Lake

Campers at Swan Lake receive beach towels to use for the day.

- Campers who stay in Campsite A receive towels that have color on exactly half of the towel.
- Campers who stay in Campsite B receive towels that have color on exactly a fourth of the towel.
- Campers who stay in Campsite C receive towels that do not have color on a half or a fourth of the towel.

At the end of each day, Swan Lake staff members must sort the towels. Can you help them sort the towels?

CCSSM Standard for Mathematical Practice

Practice 7: Look for and make use of structure.

CCSSM Standard for Mathematical Content

2.G.A.3: Partition circles and rectangles into two, three, or four equal shares, describe the shares using the words *halves, thirds, half of*, a *third of*, etc., and describe the whole as *two halves, three thirds, four fourths*. Recognize that equal shares of identical wholes need not have the same shape.

Problem Discussion

This task focuses on the early development of fraction knowledge, as students are asked to recognize fractional parts of a whole when the whole has been partitioned into equal-size pieces, or shares (Van de Walle, Karp, and Bay-Williams 2013). Students are asked to describe equal shares using words like *halves* (*half of*), *fourths* (*fourth of*), and *quarters* (*quarter of*) as well as describe the *whole* as two or four of the equal shares (2.G.A.3). Additionally, students need to recognize that equal shares of the same whole do not have to be next to each other, such as figure A, or even the same shape, such as figure B (2.G.A.3). Building on recognition of familiar images of halves and fourths, this task requires students to notice when the whole has been partitioned into equal parts. Some students may count all parts and shaded parts regardless of whether or not the shares are equal (Battista 2012; Chval, Lannin, and Jones 2013).

In figure A, students may mentally "move" one shaded part and see that half of the shape is shaded (SMP 7). In figure B, students must describe how to transform the different portions into the same shapes to recognize the structure of four equal shares making up the whole (SMP 7). Through small-group and whole-class discussions embedded in the task, students will be given the opportunity to investigate whether the whole is partitioned into equal-size parts.

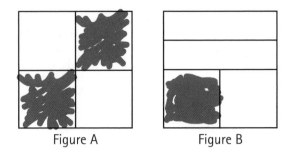

Figure A   Figure B

STRATEGIES

- Students may sort the towels that have familiar representations of halves and fourths.
- Students may sort shapes based on one part of two or four equal-size parts being colored.
- Students may cut apart the towels to determine which shapes show the appropriate fractional amount.

MISCONCEPTIONS/STUDENT DIFFICULTIES

- Students may only recognize familiar representations of halves and fourths.
- Students may count total parts and the shaded parts, neglecting the need for the parts to be of equal size.
- Students may not recognize that equal shares of the same whole do not need to have the same shape.
- Students may need to cut apart the towels to check to see if shares of different shapes are equal in area.
- Students may not see that fourths may be equivalent to a half unless the shaded parts are side by side.
- Students may struggle to understand the qualification for the towels for Campsite C campers.

LAUNCH

Show students the four images on the next page. Ask them to describe what they see to a partner. Encourage students to use terms like *halves* and *half of* and to describe the *whole* as two of the equal shares. Likewise, encourage students to use terms like *fourths*, *quarters*, *fourth of*, and *quarter of* and to describe the *whole* as four of the equal shares.

Ask these questions to check for understanding:

- Have you ever had to share equal-size pieces of something?
- How many equal shares does this shape have?
- How can you tell the portions are equal?
- Which shares are larger, half of the whole or a quarter of the whole? How do you know?

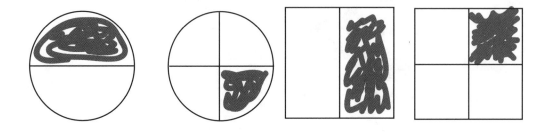

EXPLORE

Read the task aloud to students. Explain to students that the Swan Lake staff would like to have a picture of the types of towels that belong to each campsite. Ask students to work with a partner, and distribute a set of the beach towels to each pair to sort into three piles. Encourage students to use language such as fourth of, half of, whole, and so forth, to explain their thinking.

Ask the following questions to check for understanding:

- How do you know this towel belongs to Campsite A (B or C)?
- How many equal shares does this towel have? How do you know?
- How do you know both of these towels represent a half (or fourth) of the whole?

If students struggle to recognize that the towels can be segmented into halves and quarters in multiple ways, ask them to predict to which campsite a towel belongs. Next, ask students to fold or cut the towel into pieces to check if the portions are indeed equal shares.

SUMMARIZE

Once students have sorted their towels, ask them to share with the class the campsite each towel belongs to and why. If students disagree about where to place a towel, have them cut out a new picture of that towel, and fold or cut along the dividing lines to determine if the pieces match. If all the pieces are congruent or have equal areas, then the towel is partitioned into equal shares. Students can then determine if the shaded region represents halves or fourths.

Students may struggle to determine if the towels opposite represent fourths because the shares are not the same shape. Students should be encouraged to cut along the dashed line and rearrange the pieces to show that each colored section would fit into each of the white sections. Therefore, they will prove that each share is indeed one-fourth of the whole towel.

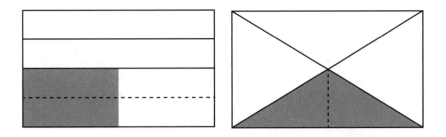

Ask students to look at all of the towels in Campsite A and determine which was the easiest towel to sort and which was the most difficult. Have students explain to a different partner why they chose those towels. Repeat this process for Campsites B and C. As a whole class, discuss what is important when trying to determine if a shape has been partitioned into halves or fourths (quarters). Be sure to highlight the fact that "equal shares of identical wholes need not have the same shape" (2.G.A.3).

DIFFERENTIATION

- For struggling students, remove some of the towels that require more developed spatial visualization skills to determine if the shares are equal in size.
- For struggling students, have precut towels for them to manipulate to check for equal areas.
- To extend the task, have students write a letter to the Swan Lake staff describing what to look for when deciding which towels go to each campsite.
- To extend the task, have students create towels with color representing *one-third of* or *one-eighth of* the towel for a new Campsite D.

LEMONADE STAND

On a hot summer day, Rakeem is running a lemonade stand in his neighborhood to raise money for the local animal shelter. He is selling lemonade for 50¢ a cup, brownies for 25¢, and cookies for 10¢ each. One customer has $1.50 and wants to spend it all. Find at least three different ways that this customer could spend all of her money. Write equations to represent your combinations and explain your reasoning.

CCSSM STANDARDS FOR MATHEMATICAL PRACTICE

Practice 4: Model with mathematics.

Practice 7: Look for and make use of structure.

CCSSM STANDARDS FOR MATHEMATICAL CONTENT

2.NBT.B.6: Add up to four two-digit numbers using strategies based on place value and properties of operations.

2.MD.C.8: Solve word problems involving dollar bills, quarter, dimes, nickels, and pennies, using $ and ¢ symbols appropriately. *Example: If you have 2 dimes and 3 pennies, how many cents do you have?*

PROBLEM DISCUSSION

In this problem, students are asked to identify three or more ways to account for $1.50 using items costing 50¢, 25¢, and 10¢. Students' problem solving during second grade involves working with coins and their values (2.MD.C.8). This problem extends that work by asking students to consider different money amounts that total $1.50. To do this, students will likely consider the costs of different quantities of the same item. For example, if one brownie costs 25¢, how much will two brownies cost? Students may use repeated addition to solve this situation (i.e., 25 + 25 = 50). They may also draw on their knowledge of the coins to determine the cost of multiple items. For example, one brownie costs a quarter; thus, two brownies costs two quarters, or 50¢. This problem may, therefore, provide students some exploratory work with multiplicative reasoning.

Students might generate tables indicating the cost of multiple items such as those on the opposite page.

Number of Cups of Lemonade	Total Cost
1	50¢
2	$1.00
3	$1.50
4	$2.00
5	$2.50
6	$3.00
7	$3.50

Number of Brownies	Total Cost
1	25¢
2	50¢
3	75¢
4	$1.00
5	$1.25
6	$1.50
7	$1.75

Number of Cookies	Total Cost
1	10¢
2	20¢
3	30¢
4	40¢
5	50¢
6	60¢
7	70¢

Tables like these may then be used to combine costs to make $1.50 by adding item quantities together on the basis of the place values involved with cent and dollar amounts (2.NBT.B.6).

Ten possible combinations are generated by adding different item quantities to make $1.50. Note that three of these combinations involve the purchase of only one type of item. The table below is an organized list of the combinations:

Number of Cups of Lemonade	Number of Brownies	Number of Cookies
3	0	0
2	2	0
2	0	5
1	4	0
1	2	5
1	0	10
0	6	0
0	4	5
0	2	10
0	0	15

Some combinations readily lend themselves as starting points for making other combinations through substitution. For instance, if the first combination is three cups of lemonade, it is possible to generate other combinations by substituting the cost of a cup of lemonade with two brownies or five cookies. Similarly, when two brownies are removed from a combination, they can be replaced with five cookies. Students may recognize and use this structure (SMP 7) to make exchanges with quantities while still maintaining equivalence.

Finally, the students are asked to model with mathematics by writing equations to represent their thinking (SMP 4). These equations may take on different forms. For example, students might represent the combination of 1 cup of lemonade, 2 brownies, and 5 cookies in the following ways:

- 1 lemonade + 2 brownies + 5 cookies = $1.50
- 50¢ + 25¢ + 25¢ + 10¢ + 10¢ + 10¢ + 10¢ + 10¢ = $1.50

Notice that in the first equation, the cost of each item is not represented. However, there is a multiplicative relationship that is implied. In the second equation, each item is represented individually by signifying its cost. Connections between the equations should be made whenever possible, and students should be able to explain how they are representing the same combination in different ways.

STRATEGIES

- Students may use coin manipulatives to find combinations of quarters and dimes that make $1.50.
- Students may use trial and error to identify combinations of 50¢, 25¢, and 10¢ that account for $1.50.
- Students may skip-count by the different values to identify how much two or more of an item would cost.
- Students may find the three combinations that involve the purchase of only one type of item by using repeated addition with the item's cost (e.g., 50¢ + 50¢ + 50¢ = $1.50).
- Students may identify the cost of multiple items of each type by making a table.
- Students may identify costs of multiple items that total $1.50 (e.g., from tables they have created) through trial and error.
- Students may identify one combination of items, and then identify two more combinations with substitutions of equivalent value for particular items (e.g., replacing two brownies with five cookies).

MISCONCEPTIONS/STUDENT DIFFICULTIES

- Students may assume that the money may only be spent on one type of item, therefore thinking that there are only three possible combinations.
- Students may assume that the customer wants at least one of each item, therefore thinking that there is only one possible combination.

- Students may "start from scratch" as they reason through each combination, rather than consider exchanging items for other items of equivalent value.
- Students may struggle with addition of values in cents and converting them to values involving more than one whole dollar.

LAUNCH

Ask students if they have ever taken part in running a lemonade stand or a bake sale. If there are students who have done so, ask them to briefly share their experiences and the types of items they sold. Ask if any of these events were run to raise money for charity, and if so, which charities they were for.

Similarly, ask students if they have every bought something at a lemonade stand or a bake sale. Have students share what items they purchased and how much they paid. This may be an opportunity to discuss the reasonableness of prices, "How much would you pay for a glass of lemonade? A brownie?"

Read the task aloud to students. Ask them to share what they know about the problem. They may identify the following facts:

- Rakeem is running a lemonade stand to raise money for his local animal shelter.
- He is charging 50¢ for lemonade, 25¢ for brownies, and 10¢ for cookies.
- A customer has $1.50 and wants to spend it all.
- There must be at least three ways to spend all the money.

List the facts that students express on the board. As needed, reread the task aloud.

Next, ask the students what they are trying to find out in the problem. Have them turn to a neighbor and share their responses. Ask for input from several students and write a corresponding question on the board.

Finally, have students think to themselves for one or two minutes about how they might go about solving this task—what is their plan? Ask them to turn to a neighbor and share their ideas. Ask the whole class if there are any lingering questions about the task and what they are supposed to do. Resolve any issues, as long as they do not lower the cognitive demand of the task itself.

EXPLORE

Have students work on the task in pairs or groups of three. Provide each group with a large piece of paper to record their three solutions and the explanations of their reasoning.

As students work, circulate throughout the room to observe and record students' thinking. Take particular note of students who are using the notion of exchange to generate equivalent expressions (e.g., exchanging one lemonade for two brownies) because this is an idea that can be highlighted in the Summarize portion of the lesson.

Ask questions like the following to check for understanding:

- How are you using the quarters and dimes to help you solve this problem?
- Why do you have some quarters paired together and others that aren't paired together?
- Can you explain how you found this combination of items that equals $1.50?
- I see that your second combination of items has some items in common with your first combination. What items do they have in common? What is different about the two combinations?
- How did you know you could substitute a lemonade for other items? Are there other substitutions you could use?
- What do your tables show you about the cost of the items that are being sold at Rakeem's lemonade stand?
- How did you use your tables to help you find combinations of items that equal $1.50?
- How do the values in your equation represent the items that the customer is buying?

If students are struggling to find a combination of items that works, ask, "Is there a way that the customer could spend all of her money by buying only lemonade?" Encourage them to use coin manipulatives as needed to represent the value of each item. Watch them as they consider this question because it may reveal challenges with different parts of the question, such as going beyond $1.00 by combining values in cents.

If students are finished finding combinations, encourage them to explain their thinking thoroughly, and write each combination as an equation. Ask groups to be prepared to present specific combinations. Record the combinations each group will present so they can be called in the order of the table provided in the Problem Discussion.

SUMMARIZE

Ask each group to come forward to explain their reasoning for the combination they have been assigned to present. Prepare a chart (opposite) to record their quantities of items that enable the customer to spend $1.50. Consider having groups present these options in order, so that the concepts of exchange and maintaining equivalence can be highlighted. To organize this, either record combinations during the Explore section of the lesson, or ask, "Are there any other groups that have a combination that involves two cups of lemonade?" For each combination, record the equation the group used to represent their thinking. If there are questions about the equation representations, address these as they surface.

Number of Cups of Lemonade	Number of Brownies	Number of Cookies	Equation
3	0	0	50¢ + 50¢ + 50¢ = $1.50 *or* 3 lemonades = $1.50

Following each group's presentation, ask students to articulate what the latest combination has in common with the preceding combination. For example, students might notice that both of the combinations have at least two cups of lemonade and no cookies. Ask, "So what was taken away from the first combination to get to the second combination? What replaced the (cup of lemonade)? Why does this make sense?" Students should begin to articulate that items are being exchanged: Items are taken away and replaced with items of equal value. As much as possible, ask students to articulate this concept of compensation in order to maintain equivalence.

If there are fewer than ten combinations after all groups have presented, ask students if they have any combinations that have not been shared. Record these. If there are still gaps, ask students if there are any additional combinations that might be generated. This conversation could be narrowly directed toward the concept of exchange. For example, "If I took away two brownies from this combination, what could I replace them with so the customer is still paying $1.50?" Add the combination(s) to the list.

Finally, ask students, "Are all of these combinations equivalent? How do we know? What does *equivalent* mean?" Students may note that the combinations all cost the same amount, so in that way they are equivalent. Ask students to think about the equations they have provided in a different way; write on the board, 50¢ + 50¢ + 50¢ = 50¢ + 25¢ + 25¢ + 10¢ + 10¢ + 10¢ + 10¢, and ask if this is a true number sentence. For students who view the equal sign as a symbol to do the computation, this may be challenging for them to interpret. Emphasize the equals sign as meaning "is the same as" so students can correctly make sense of this equation.

DIFFERENTIATION

- If students struggle to work toward a particular value, present a few combinations of items for them to figure out first, such as 1 cup of lemonade, 1 brownie, and 2 cookies.
- The number of items available for purchase can be reduced to two, either lemonade and brownies or lemonade and cookies.
- For students who struggle to go beyond one dollar with values provided in cents, change the amount that the customer has to spend to a value below one dollar, such as 90¢, and reduce the number of combinations they need to identify.

- Challenge students by changing the amount of money the customer wants to spend to a nonmultiple of ten, such as $1.45.
- Challenge students by asking questions like the following regarding the possibility of different combinations:
    - Is it possible for the customer to purchase three brownies?
    - Is it possible for the customer to purchase an odd number of brownies?
    - Is it possible for the customer to purchase three cookies as part of a combination? (This question could be asked of any number that is not a multiple of five.)
    - Is it possible for the customer to purchase at least one of each item?
    - Is it possible for the customer to spend only $1.45 of her money?
- Extend the task by asking students to find all possible combinations of items that would account for $1.50.
- Challenge students to find dollar-and-cent amounts that cannot be completely spent by a customer.

REFERENCES

Battista, M. T. *Cognitive-Based Assessment & Teaching of Fractions: Building On Students' Reasoning.* Portsmouth, N.H.: Heinemann, 2012.

Battista, M. T. *Cognitive-Based Assessment & Teaching of Place Value: Building On Students' Reasoning.* Portsmouth, N.H.: Heinemann, 2012.

Caldwell, J. H., K. Karp, and J. M. Bay-Williams. *Developing Essential Understanding of Addition and Subtraction: Pre-K–Grade 2.* Reston, Va.: National Council of Teachers of Mathematics, 2011.

Chval, K., J. Lannin, and D. Jones. *Putting Essential Understanding of Fractions into Practice: 3–5.* Reston, Va.: National Council of Teachers of Mathematics, 2013.

Clements, D. H. "Subitizing: What Is It? Why Teach It?" *Teaching Children Mathematics 5*, no. 7, (1999): 400–405.

Clements, D. H., and J. Sarama. "Early Childhood Mathematics Learning." In *Second Handbook of Research on Mathematics Teaching and Learning*, edited by F. K. Lester, Jr., pp. 461–555. New York: Information Age Publishing, 2007.

Clements, D. H., and J. Sarama. *Learning and Teaching Early Math: The Learning Trajectories Approach.* New York: Routledge, 2009.

Common Core Standards Writing Team. "Front Matter" and "Grades K–6, Geometry." In *Progressions for the Common Core State Standards in Mathematics (draft).* Tucson, Ariz.: Institute for Mathematics and Education, University of Arizona, 2013.

Dougherty, B., A. Flores, E. Louis, C. Sophian, and R. Zbiek. *Developing Essential Understanding of Number and Numeration for Teaching Mathematics in Pre-K–2.* Reston, Va.: National Council of Teachers of Mathematics, 2010.

Eves, H. *A Survey Of Geometry: Volume 1.* Boston: Allyn and Bacon, 1963.

Fuson, K. C., D. Clements, and S. Beckmann. *Focus In Pre-K: Teaching with Curriculum Focal Points.* Reston, Va.: National Council of Teachers of Mathematics, 2010.

Friederwitzer, F. J. and B. Berman. "The Language of Time." *Teaching Children Mathematics 6*, no. 4, (1999): 254–259.

Hiebert, J. "Signposts for Teaching Mathematics through Problem Solving." In *Teaching Mathematics through Problem Solving: Prekindergarten–Grade 6*, edited by J. Frank K. Lester, pp. 53–61. Reston, Va.: National Council of Teachers of Mathematics, 2003.

Lappan, G., E. D. Phillips, J. T. Fey, and S. N. Friel. *Connected Mathematics Project*, 3rd ed. Developed at Michigan State University. Boston: Pearson Prentice Hall, 2014.

McCloskey, R. *Make Way for Ducklings.* New York: The Viking Press, 1941.

Moomaw, S. *Teaching Mathematics in Early Childhood.* Baltimore, Md.: Brookes Publishing, 2011.

National Council of Teachers of Mathematics. *Principles and Standards for School Mathematics.* Reston, Va.: National Council of Teachers of Mathematics, 2000.

National Council of Teachers of Mathematics. *Curriculum Focal Points for Prekindergarten through Grade 8 Mathematics.* Reston, Va.: National Council of Teachers of Mathematics, 2006.

National Governors Association Center for Best Practices (NGA Center) and Council of Chief State School Officers (CCSSO). *Common Core State Standards for Mathematics*. Washington, D.C.: NGA Center and CCSSO, 2010. http://www.corestandards.org.

Tobey, C. R., and E. R. Fagan. *Uncovering Student Thinking about Mathematics in the Common Core, Grades K–2: 20* Formative Assessment Probes. Thousand Oaks, Calif.: Corwin, 2013.

Van de Walle, J. A. "Designing and Selecting Problem-Based Tasks." In *Teaching Mathematics through Problem Solving: Prekindergarten–Grade 6*, edited by J. Frank K. Lester, pp. 67–80. Reston, Va.: National Council of Teachers of Mathematics, 2003.

Van de Walle, J. A., K. S. Karp, and J. M. Bay-Williams. *Elementary and Middle School Mathematics: Teaching Developmentally*. 7th edition. Boston: Pearson Education, Inc., 2010.

Van de Walle, J. A., K. S. Karp, and J. M. Bay-Williams. *Elementary and Middle School Mathematics: Teaching Developmentally*. 8th edition. Boston: Pearson Education, Inc., 2013.

van Hiele, P. M. "Developing Geometric Thinking through Activities that Begin with Play." *Teaching Children Mathematics 5* no. 6, (1999): 310–313.

Zietz, P. *The Art And Craft of Problem Solving*. New York: Wiley, 1999.